A THOUSAND PAPER CUTS

A Thousand Paper Cuts
Copyright © 2024 by Heather Boorman-Morris, MSW, LCSW

All rights reserved under the Pan-American and International Copyright Conventions. This book may not be reproduced in whole or in part, except for brief quotations embodied in critical articles or reviews, in any form or by any means, electronic or mechanical, including photocopying, recording, or by any information storage and retrieval system now known or hereinafter invented, without written permission of the publisher, Armin Lear Press.

Library of Congress Control Number: 2023951228

ISBN (paperback): 978-1-956450-95-8
ISBN (Ebook): 978-1-956450-96-5

Armin Lear Press, Inc.
215 W Riverside Drive, #4362
Estes Park, CO 80517

A THOUSAND PAPER CUTS

A Therapist, Her Narcissist, His Trap

Heather Boorman-Morris, MSW, LCSW

To Rachel, Katie, & my mom,
who bandaged the cuts as I fell apart.

And to Antwan,
who loved my scars into beautiful healing.

Contents

Part 1   A Thousand Paper Cuts   1

Part 2   The Awakening   97

Part 3   Freedom   167

Acknowledgments   211

About the Author   213

PART 1

A Thousand Paper Cuts

Forty-Two Years

How did I get here? Clinging to the edge of the king-sized bed, trying to make myself as small as I could. Curled on my side, knees tucked up to my chest, hands gripping the mattress piping, frozen. How did I get here? A silent tear fell from my right eye, dripped over the bridge of my nose and into my left eye. I prayed that my tears would go unseen. I prayed that the person next to me wouldn't notice. I couldn't move. I couldn't make a noise. I couldn't remember how I got here.

I knew the situation immediately before this silent terror, devoid of everything intimate and warm. I remembered that clearly. But I could not remember the steps in my life that brought me to this place. How did the little girl who dreamed of becoming the first female quarterback of the Green Bay Packers become this soul-weary, lonely, middle-aged woman?

It couldn't have happened suddenly. I would have noticed that. I would have seen the dementor's kiss approaching and I would have dodged it, or at least remembered it.

It couldn't have been my choice. I would never have chosen this crowded, lonely cave. I would have chosen to be alone for eternity over this.

I could not have been aware of what was happening.

Had I seen it, had I been able to understand it, I would have left long ago.

Yet, somehow, it happened. Somehow, despite my compassion, intelligence, independence, and ambition, despite the success I had achieved in life, I lay balanced on the edge of the bed unable to move. Since this couldn't have been my conscious choice, it must have been a subtle, long and winding road that brought me to this place. Here I didn't know what joy and love *were* let alone feel them. I thought I knew the love of happily ever after, but pages of silent terror were embedded deep inside the fairy tale that I mistook for reality. The fairy tale that the man sleeping next to me had so carefully crafted. The fairy tale that I clung to as fiercely as I clung to that mattress piping because I couldn't believe it wasn't true. A fairy tale that started one beautiful summer in Maine.

Twenty-Two Years

"It feels so good to be able to think solely of myself and what I want!"

The car windows were down. The mixtape pumped out the soundtrack of our cross-country road trip. With a smile on my face, hair blowing into my mouth, and freedom in my heart I thrust my arm out the window and felt the wind jostle it and jolt it from one spot to another.

Nine months earlier my first and only long-term romantic relationship had ended. It ended while I sat at a communal phone in the hallway with my new fellow students walking past me with questioning eyes as they saw my tears. I was listening to a voice thousands of miles away tell me he wanted to put our relationship on hold. "No. You don't put four and a half years on hold," I'd said. And so we were done.

As my friend drove us on the interstates and backcountry roads from Ohio to Maine, I recognized my heart had healed enough that I could simply relish in the independence and freedom. No one to consider other than my very own self.

"I could join the Peace Corps if I want! I could just go backpacking across the continent! I could do anything!"

The punchline that has traditionally followed my retelling of this tale goes something like this: "Yeah. I was engaged by the end of the summer."

This would be followed by knowing smiles and comments like "when you know, you know!" Twenty years later, as my fingertips are still sore from the intense grip on the edge of the mattress, the punchline doesn't seem so sweet.

My friend and I were headed to a summer camp. We had just celebrated our graduation from college and were looking forward to one last carefree summer working as camp counselors together before we had to face reality, get real jobs, and commence adulting.

We pulled into the small Quaker camp after dark. Unfamiliar places look ominous in the dark. After hesitantly peering through the car windows to see what can only be described as a sketchy, abandoned, clusterfuck of primitive, graffitied cabins, we nearly turned around and drove off into the wilds of Maine where our survival would certainly be more assured.

Alas, we were both people-pleasers and rule followers and parking the car was truly our only option. Turns out the camp wasn't completely abandoned. The art cabin harbored five or six twenty-somethings who seemed oddly incongruous with typical camp staffers. More artsy than outdoorsy, more grungy than tree-huggy, these veteran counselors apparently did belong to the camp and made it clear that they belonged more than my friend and I did. Looking back, I can't blame them. They were reuniting after months of not seeing each other and naturally preferred reconnecting with their friends to showing strangers around the dark, wooded camp outside.

After only a few minutes and a few thousand regretful and homesick thoughts, we slipped out the meetinghouse door in search of friendlier faces or an exit plan. As if by magic, a rickety green van, filled with smiling faces, pulled into the camp's gravel entrance. People piled off the van and friendly greetings ensued. The group of us went into the dining hall, flipping the light switch as we entered and, in one beautiful moment, the building, the room, the faces and my outlook all brightened.

As I reflect back now, he met me at the perfect time in my life. I was an ambitious young social worker, a service-minded person filled with energy, optimism and compassion. I was two weeks past my college graduation at which I earned a BA with double majors, double minors, honors college recognition and a GPA warranting the standing ovation summa cum laude students were awarded. I was confident and embraced my accomplishments and intellect. I relished my independence and strong-willed determination to save the world.

And yet, I was only a couple of years out of an eating disorder, extraordinarily insecure about my body, attractiveness and ability to find a suitable partner who would want to partner with me. I was vulnerable in a state I didn't know, at a camp I was scared to be at and surrounded by strangers. Part of me was desperately reaching out for protective arms to reassure and guide me.

With my blend of confidence, insecurity and whimpering tolerance, I was essentially a parasitic supply source. Yes, he met me at a perfect time. For him.

Somehow, almost immediately, I found myself in a group of other new counselors with whom I knew, from the beginning, I wouldn't be spending the summer. Sure, we'd be at the camp together, but the spark of friendship was missing. Being an overly kind young person, I didn't know how to excuse myself and so I stayed in that circle while regularly glancing across the room to the group of people my friend had landed with. The group of people I was certain were more my style. One guy in that group would regularly be glancing right back at me.

I wasn't initially attracted to him and I wasn't trying to catch his eye. In truth, his curly haired, bohemian friend, with his joyful and easy smile, tugged at my spirit far more than he did. My soul felt a sense of comfort and home with that laid back, easy-going, quietly friendly and creative man. That's the type of man, I imagine, who would have provided a far better place for my soul to rest, but he was not the one who rescued me. He did not pursue me. He remained his quiet, steady self while I was wooed by the tall, attractive, cool guy that part of me never believed I could attract.

Suddenly, this tall white knight leaned over to my friend, obviously asked her for my name, and then looked straight at me and called my name. With an English accent. That little girl in me who wanted protecting felt seen and rescued. I scooted away from the group of friendly non-friends and the dance began.

The dance in which he flashed his George Clooney eyes; when he dipped his head and bashfully looked up at me through his eyelashes with just the right amount of mischievous twinkle to be intriguing. The dance in which he tested out compliments and observed my inability to accept them; displayed traditional chivalry and English charm; made me laugh and playfully enticed me. The dance in which he studied me and listened so intently to my words that he became familiar with every aspect of my complicated self. His self-deprecating humor begged for an uplifting response and his sweet moments of vulnerability drew me in.

Forty-Two Years

It's been a long time since I've seen his Clooney eyes. Is that how it started? When the natural attention of infatuation faded and his eyes became normal, everyday eyes? Instead of the mattress, was I actually clinging to the memory of his Clooney eyes? How did I go from feeling so obsessively desired to being so achingly alone?

The compliments still come. When they are useful. The familiarity with me is so deep that I regularly underestimate just how well he knows me inside and out. I see the chivalry. I hear the English accent. I watch them partner to convince and charm those around him. I miss being the recipient. Is that why I'm clinging? Because I want to receive that charming attention again? Because I'm desperately missing it, trying to figure out what I did to make it go away?

Five Years

I grew up in a small town in Western Wisconsin. Today it is a suburb of Minneapolis and St Paul, but when I was a child, Hudson was small, quaint and unhurried. Nestled between the bluffs and the banks of the St Croix River, my town boasted of a drive-up A&W, complete with roller skating carhops; a couple of bars; one grocery store, called Red Owl, that had a giant, angry looking owl head hanging over the front door; a bowling alley; several churches; some decent schools, and a movie theater.

The theater could show one movie at a time and its sloped seating led downward to the curtained stage and large screen. The seats, upholstered in ratty, red velvet, folded down and dilapidated springs poked into the worn fabric. Feet either crunched popcorn or stuck to the soda-soaked floor. I think they could only afford one new release a year, so the theater mostly played classics and second run films. It was magnificent.

At five, I always sat in an obstructed seat. I couldn't get around it because I wasn't tall enough to see over the seats in front of me, much less the hairy heads above the seatbacks. And so, I would keep my seat folded up and precariously balance on the edge of it, occasionally collapsing back to obstructed view when my excited little body squirmed a bit too much.

It was in this theater that I saw the animated classic *Bambi* and first understood the irritation children in movie theaters could bring. A girl behind me could not stop crying after Bambi's mom died. So annoying. Leave if you can't be quiet!

And it was in this theater that I saw *Snow White* and *Cinderella*. I loved the music. I loved the stories. I loved the little singing men and the mice that pitched in to help. Gus-Gus was my favorite. I also loved the princes, the romance of balls and love's true kisses. I especially loved men willing to traipse throughout the countryside with a fragile shoe until they found their one true love. I fell in love with the fairy tale and out of touch with reality.

Seventeen Years

He was nice enough. That guy who broke up with me on a shared public phone. We were friends for a long time at first and talked every night. He professed that he like-liked me in a letter. It was sweet. We went to the prom and did all the expected things: flowers, fancy car, dinner out, dance, sleepover at a friend's place and waffles in the morning. It was fun. It was ordinary.

Everything about this relationship was ordinary. No glass slippers, no dancing mice, no swooning and grandiose romantic gestures. He was fine. I knew I loved him, but he was no Prince Charming and I knew that, too.

Twenty-Two Years

The first week of camp life was magical. My friend and I woke in the morning and the camp itself looked far less like the setting for *Summer Serial Killers* and far more like the traditional summer camp we had signed up for. Days were filled with camp preparedness, first aid training, get-to-know-you icebreakers and, for us newbies, learning traditional camp games. The nights were filled with flirtations and alcohol and cigarettes and parties at a nearby lake. Kids wouldn't arrive for another week and we counselors lived the camp life without much responsibility.

Being young and ridiculous, he and I would stay up all night talking, teasing, and laughing. We would get an hour or two of sleep, drag ourselves to morning meeting and start the process all over again, promising we wouldn't stay up so late again that night only to be swept away in our flirtations and conversations and refusal to be apart.

He listened intently. He asked probing questions. I felt interesting and listened to, desirable and connected. I looked at him and saw thoughtfulness, caring, deep conversation and emotions that far surpassed those of the men and boys I'd known before. He would talk about himself when I asked, but was far more interested in learning about me, understanding my viewpoints, appreciating the way I thought and the opinions I had.

At one point during that week his 6'4" frame slammed down on my face and nose as he competitively jumped in the air to catch a disc his teammate threw in a fierce game of ultimate frisbee. Just like in a cartoon, I saw stars and dropped to the ground. Immediately my lip began to swell, my nose bled, and my head throbbed. He profusely apologized, called our resident paramedic over to assess the situation and ran off to grab an icepack. I was fine and I was smitten. In truth, seeing that aggressive desire to win heightened my attraction.

He took great care of me. This twenty-one-year-old man opted out of the group plans to lay by me and hold the ice pack. He would glance at me during the staff meeting later that day and whisper apologies from across the room.

The night before kids invaded the camp, all the counselors went out for a meal. We shared excitements and worries. When we got back to camp, the others went off to their cabins and he and I stayed outside. He asked me to walk with him and we found ourselves on a deck outside the director's empty office. We knew we were going to kiss before the evening ended. Finally, after three hours, he held out his hand, bit his bottom lip and told me to sit near him. Like the best movie moment kisses, he held my face gently in his hands, gazed into my eyes, glanced down at my lips and then kissed me. It was deliciously sweet.

The next morning he came into my cabin. I lay on the top bunk and when he approached we were eye to eye.

"How are you doing?" he asked.

"Nervous," I said.

He agreed that I must be nervous, given that my trust had been broken from my last relationship. He listened, reassuring and validating me, and his eyes twinkled as he told me that we'd be fine.

"We just need to keep communicating," he said. "So long as we're communicating, we'll be fine." Kissing me quickly, Prince Charming then walked out the door.

Twenty-Three Years

We're sitting in the Piggly Wiggly parking lot. I can't remember what led to the argument, but I do remember we were parked a few spots down from the overhead light and shadowed in darkness.

"Are you crying again?" he asked. I couldn't identify it at the time, but his question oozed with disgust and my insides responded with twisting, nauseating angst.

I didn't answer. I just sniffed.

I had been crying a lot; my days were marked with more tears than smiles. I was ashamed. I felt I deserved the tone. Somehow, we just weren't doing this marriage thing right. Older adults would ask how the newlyweds were faring with a wink-wink, nudge-nudge. I would smile bashfully back and respond with a pleasantry while inside I felt like a fraud. It was awful. I couldn't put my finger on it, but something felt off.

It was probably just because he was adapting to a new country and living away from his family.

It was probably just because I had unreasonable expectations of what married life would be.

It was probably just because finances were strained as I worked at a non-profit and he was unable to work until his visa came through.

It was probably just because we were working out the bugs of two people with two different ways of doing things coming together to find their one way of doing things.

It was probably just because we were adulting for the first time.

It was probably just because it was his first real winter.

It was probably just because I was overly persnickety about certain things.

It was probably just because our 80-year-old landlord who lived downstairs would regularly let himself and his two giant dogs into our apartment when we weren't there.

It was probably just because of a great many things and I specialized in finding all the reasons.

Back in the Piggly Wiggly parking lot, silently crying in the dark, I sat in the driver's seat and looked down at my hands.

"I can't believe you are crying again. I married you because you're one of the strong ones and seemed put together."

Thirty-Three Years

Being a therapist engenders interesting relationships. We care, but need to care in a professional manner—at least inside the therapy room and in our interactions with you. We can't speak to you the same way we'd speak to a friend. We need to measure our words to ensure that they maintain professional boundaries without being stiff. Truthfully, though, the good ones? We care a lot. And we probably care about you far more than we can completely let on in our sessions. It isn't just a job for us. We don't care because we're paid to, despite many an attachment-impaired teens' claims to the contrary. No, we care because we are human, and often empathic humans who have endured our own struggles and want our pain to birth freedom, growth, and comfort in others.

My heart ached as I listened to the enormously sad news a group member was telling me over the phone.

I had been working at an intensive outpatient program, providing group and individual therapy to some of the most at-risk people. These were people who had just been discharged from a psychiatric hospitalization or were at risk of needing a hospitalization. These were people for whom suicide always seemed to be an option. We rejoiced when they made it to group because managing anxiety sufficiently to be able to leave the house was an extraordinary accomplishment.

One of my younger group members, for whom I provided one hour of individual therapy and nine hours of group therapy a week, had died. Unexpectedly.

I'd facilitated a lot of grief in my years as a therapist and in a therapeutic group. But one of my favorite patients, a woman who was only in her early 40s, had died suddenly and I was devastated. My heart ached. And yet, I was on the phone with another one of my patients. So, I took a breath, shook off the shock, and provided comfort and therapy.

I took another breath, poured some coffee and walked into the room where ten expectant group members waited for me to deliver the news.

To sit with another person's grief while you are grieving is one of the hardest tasks I've been asked to do as a therapist. After my dad died, I had many, MANY sessions in which I had to set my own grief aside to be present for the emotions of the person in front of me. To sit with ten people grieving the same person while I also grieved that loss? There simply are no words. But I did it. I did not fall apart. I set my own stuff aside, showed up for the people in the room who needed me, empathized, commiserated, found hope, and sought supervision and support from my coworkers.

At the end of the day, I drove home and sat on the couch. I looked at my husband sitting off to my right and told him about my day. I could finally release my tears.

"Oh," he said flatly. "That sucks."

I sniffed.

He said, "I mean, at least she was just a patient, so it should be easy to get through."

I looked up and shook my head.

He made a joke. I don't remember the joke, but I know

he made it. I know he made it because I remember this incident, and because he always made a joke in situations like this. Nothing could be serious until he decided it was.

"It's ok for me to be sad right now," I said. "Please don't try to make me feel better."

He said, "Well, I guess it's just too hard for me to watch you in pain, so if you feel like you need to cry you probably shouldn't do it in front of me."

So I left and cried alone in my room.

Thirty-Five Years

I received a phone call in the middle of the night. It was eight hours before we were going to deposit our two children on their grandparents' doorstep and get away for the weekend. Instead, I drove to my mom's at one in the morning on June 23, 2012. My mom had woken to find my dad unconscious in the kitchen. She said the paramedics were there now. I said I was on my way and asked if I should go to the house or the hospital. The paramedics said to the house.

And that's how I learned my dad had died.

I spent the next thirty minutes dressing, driving and dreaming up reasons the paramedics could have told me to go to the house other than that my dad was already dead. The dark, silent, and slow-moving ambulance driving away from my parents' home confirmed what I already knew.

My dad was 62. He wasn't in great health, but as far as the rest of us knew he didn't have any terminal illness either. His death was a surprise. I would cry every time someone commented about my pregnant belly during the funeral. My father would never meet my youngest child. He was born less than three months after my father's death.

My patients needed their therapist and this therapist needed money and insurance and some sense of normalcy, so a week after we buried my dad, I returned to work.

A month after we buried my dad, I called my husband. I was driving from the job I had facilitating groups at a hospital to my private practice. I had a few clients that evening and was already burnt out with grief. He had something to go to that night, so I called him to tell him I needed the kids to be in bed before I got there. My pregnant body was tired. I was experiencing Braxton Hicks contractions. My grief was ready to explode from my body through either unending tears or irritated snark. I didn't have the energy to be patient with my young children.

"Of course. No problem. Whatever I can do to help."

I arrived home. He and my two children were in the kitchen. He was yelling. Kids were crying. I came in, sighed and sarcastically said "thanks" under my breath.

He turned his anger on me. He blamed me for running late. He yelled something about how he saw my car in the parking lot when it wasn't supposed to be there. He yelled that he didn't have time to deal with "this cluster" and that he was going to be late. I said "fine", told him to leave and prepped the kids for bed.

By the time he returned home my eyes were burning from crying and my body ached with exhaustion. I lay in bed watching braindead television. He came into the bedroom and, without a word, began changing into pajamas.

I said, "I don't understand. I can understand if things went awry and you couldn't get the kids to bed. Things happen. I don't understand how you could start yelling at me on a night when I'd specifically asked for extra gentleness."

He responded, "I just felt so bad that I wasn't able to give you what you asked for."

"Well, I understand that sometimes your worry comes out as anger, but that needs to change. It made a bad day worse. I can understand that anger is your easy emotion and worry or disappointment in yourself is uncomfortable for you. But I need you to work on it."

"Of course I will. I know it isn't right, but it's just what happens. I felt horrible and then when you were running late it just made me even more frustrated and I took it out on you."

His words were so smooth that I didn't see them for what they were. It sounded like an apology. It sounded like empathy. I didn't hear that he never actually said he was sorry. I didn't hear that he said his anger was my fault for being late. I didn't hear what he was actually offering: a fauxpology and blame wrapped up in squishy words to resemble remorse, but without feeling.

Twenty-Two Years
I overheard the camp director telling someone that the English guy must really like me because he had never spent this much time on a camper before. Giddy that he "really

liked me," I missed that he didn't like the kids as much as he seemed to.

The boy was eight years old. It was the first two-week session of camp. We had been told before his arrival that his parents were most likely going to be giving him to the foster care system after camp. They just "couldn't deal with him anymore." His sister, also at the camp, would be going home.

This was my kind of kid. I root for the underdogs. I seek out the ones who feel less loved or worthy and seem weirder and more troublesome. I can see beneath the behavior and find the softer spots. I feel compassion rather than anger.

His parents weren't wrong. This kid had some pretty significant behaviors. I was drawn to him. That first week of the session I found ways to minimize his aggression and teach him new ways. The English guy, of course, was regularly by my side. In truth, we were both neglecting our own cabins, but we had co-counselors and they were doing fine. My heart melted as he was drawn to find the good in this kid, too.

By the end of the first day the boy cuddled up in my lap. He would walk hand-in-hand with us across the camp. He would try on my glasses and hat and smile contentedly, snuggled between the English counselor and me.

On one occasion we snuck away to get him a secret treat. The English guy and I were flirting all the while but trying to be discreet. Campers were not supposed to know about the lurid affairs of their counselors.

He said something about me not even liking him.

The kid said, "Yeah, she does. You can see it in her eyes."
And he knew he had me.
I'm sure he knew he had me before that.
Two nights earlier we had been out on night patrol. We walked around the camp ensuring everyone was in bed and not up to shenanigans while the other counselors, who had gotten off an hour before, headed to their bunks. That first session was filled with younger campers, so it was less likely to be shenanigans and more likely to be homesickness and tears.

We rounded the corner to find "our" kid out of his cabin, crying.

"I can't fall asleep," he said.

We walked him back into the cabin, careful not to disturb the soft murmurs and sleep-heavy breathing of his cabinmates. I tucked him in, gave him a hug, and turned to leave.

The 6'4" man I was smitten with squatted next to this heartbroken boy and told him a softly voiced story. *Pete's Day* he called it. He ran through the events of this child's day, from the breakfast bell to the prediction of a peaceful night's sleep packed with pleasant dreams. The English voice calmed as the story went on. He stroked his hair gently, and our boy's lids began to close.

As I watched from the doorway, my heart flipped, and I knew I was falling in love.

Years later my friend told me that he had told her about this story. He said he was very aware I was watching him. He admitted he'd told *Pete's Day* to win me over.

Thirty-One Years

The eyes. There's an intensity in the eyes. A hatred. A seething rage. The eyes are enough to throw your stomach into a somersault and your heart into your throat. The eyes can make you shrink.

That's the effect the eyes had on me—a 5'8" adult woman who generally knows I'm not at fault.

The eyes targeted my three-year-old son. I couldn't imagine what it felt like to be staring up at this ginormous person with a deep voice and raging eyes. Through gritted teeth his dad sneered, "I don't care. You shouldn't be down here. You're going to wake your sister."

My son had awoken from a bad dream. He came down because he was scared. I would only find this out later because his dad immediately yelled and glared when he heard the creaking stairs of our old home. No pause to figure out why the preschooler had come downstairs. No concern for his son or daughter. He simply didn't want to be inconvenienced by a baby awakening in the night.

I stepped in front of my husband, picked my son up, rubbed his back and carried him up to his room. I listened to his dream. I validated his fear. I hugged his tiny little three-year-old body.

And then I told him *My Son's Day* in a soft voice until he forgot about the eyes and fell asleep.

Twenty-Two Years

Our first date took place two weeks after our first kiss and involved a tattoo, a meal, a dance, and a hotel room.

I'd always lived life in the expected way. I did well in school. I went to college. I did well in college. I followed the rules and I never talked back.

At 22, I wanted to do something unexpected. So, I got my first tattoo. I'm such a rebel.

He went with me and helped me pick out a sweet little giraffe face. I wanted it on the back of my left shoulder, so I straddled the artist's chair facing my date. He gazed lovingly at me as I winced with the pain of the black outlining. He let me squeeze his hands and seemed to be happy to be my rock.

At one point the artist's wife saw my shoulder and said, "Oh, what a cute camel . . . not a camel . . . it's a . . . a . . . a giraffe! Why couldn't I remember the name?!" I gave my date the sign to take a look. He gave the nod of approval and with a laugh I said, "Lucky for you it's not a camel! I've got a 6'4" Englishman with me as my bodyguard!" Later he would say he loved being my protector.

After the tattoo we went to eat. He slyly led me away from the restaurant doors, however, and into a bookstore. He sat me down in the children's section and grabbed a particular book. He returned, knelt before me and read *Guess How Much I Love You*. His English accent, the sweet inflections, the mischievous smile, the kiss on the back of my hand . . . I swooned. It was straight out of a romance novel.

When he finished the story, we noticed a Winnie the Pooh section. I explained that Eeyore had always been my favorite character. I wanted to give that donkey a hug. Without me noticing, he bought a little book with a stuffed Eeyore attached. Up until we had children, there wasn't a night I didn't have either the Englishman or Eeyore sleeping in the bed beside me.

A nice meal later we began walking out to the car. The speakers outside the restaurant sang of love and romance. He grabbed my hands and began leading me in a dance. In the middle of the parking lot, stars and moon glowing overhead. Eeyore in my pocket. Englishman holding me, whispering sweetness, pulling me close and dancing. It was the stuff of fairy tales.

My first boyfriend and I had waited nearly four years before we had intercourse. I had grown up believing I'd wait until marriage.

My English prince became my second sexual partner. I had known him for an entire three weeks.

Forty-Two Years

I lay frozen on the side of the bed and my muscles tightened into the fetal position. Three weeks after meeting the man lying next to me I spent the night unclothed, but didn't feel naked. Twenty years later, all the clothing in the world would not have helped me feel covered.

Five Years

I stood alone in a basement laundry room. On the table in front of me lay the stack of clean handkerchiefs I'd pulled from the dryer.

I remember being frightened walking down the artificially lit corridor. I remember being frightened of the woman walking with a skunk on a leash. Years later, my adult mind is unsure if the skunk was actually a skunk, but I *was* a five-year-old alone in an apartment building's downstairs laundry room dutifully folding my dad's handkerchiefs just the way he liked them.

I'm not sure how it happened, but I knew from a very early age that you simply didn't say no to my dad. I couldn't tell him I was too afraid to do something. What he said went. Any refusal would be met with something I feared. For certain there'd be the look. Often there'd be a rough and diminishing voice. But by the time I had attained narrative memory, I had already learned not to disagree, so I really don't know what would have happened if I had.

I do know that I was five and down in the scary basement folding his handkerchiefs because I knew I couldn't say no.

I know that I would regularly wind up getting his ice water, making his coffee, giving him a backrub because I knew I couldn't say no.

I also know that I kept my mouth shut and my opinions to myself.

And I know that this generalized into insecurity and timidity around all boys and men.

Eighteen Years

We were home from college on some sort of break. The family had gone to bed and we were lying next to each other on the couch, watching a movie.

His hand slid under the blanket before he turned to face me.

We wouldn't have intercourse for another two years, but "virgin" is a label many of us (formerly) conservative Christians owned with a whole lot of loopholes and workarounds. I was once told that the longer couples withhold genital penetration, the more creative their sex lives will be.

As he turned toward me, I knew what he was expecting. I knew he wanted all the jobs and that he wanted to get me to an orgasm.

But I was tired. I wasn't interested.

I told him so.

He put on a pouty face and said please.

I told him I wasn't in the mood.

He started kissing my neck and asked if he could get me in the mood.

I told him I was tired and didn't want to.

He told me to relax and it'd been a while.

I sighed.

He touched.

I didn't say no.

But I also didn't say yes.

Twenty Years

"However we dress, wherever we go, yes means yes and no means no!"

"However we dress, wherever we go, yes means yes and no means no!"

At least a hundred men and women surrounded me as we marched through campus, around the neighboring streets, and finally up fraternity row. United against violence, we marched to Take Back the Night. A few people threw bottles and cigarette butts at us and shouted drunken, lewd slurs, but most people were supportive. One fraternal society, however, was decidedly not.

I'd supported friends who'd been raped. I understood patriarchy and was beginning to claim my own independence and power. I understood how my eating disorder had been influenced by many things, one of which was most definitely misogyny. I was a big advocate for women's rights.

As we shouted that yes means yes and no means no, I felt it whole heartedly. I shouted with passion, which was unusual for a woman as typically quiet as I was.

I imagined women held at knifepoint.

I imagined women being held down by men who were stronger than they were.

I imagined clothes being torn off, tears being shed, screams shifting from forceful refusals to soft whimpers of resignation.

I thought of my friends who'd been cornered by dates. Friends who'd been stalked. Friends who felt terrified.

I shouted for these women. I shouted for the millions of women who lived with the terror of sexual assault. I shouted for the women who experienced hypervigilance, nightmares, fear and shame. I shouted for the women whose No was ignored. I shouted for the women who were acutely aware they had been raped.

In this powerful and important protest, the silent women were still silenced. The women who were raped without violent threats were quieted. The women who simply felt hollow, foggy, alone or used after a "sexual" encounter were left to feel hollow and alone.

We protested violence.

We protested patriarchy.

We protested rape.

Yes means yes and no means no.

But what about those who said nothing?

Twenty-Two Years

Engaging in a new fling while working as a camp counselor takes some creativity and stealth.

Unless we were on night patrol, we had exactly two hours a day when we were not with campers. The first was during quiet time when we had a staff meeting. The second was for an hour after camper bedtimes when we were free to do as we pleased.

We quickly began scheduling our free nights at the same time. This wasn't always possible and the nights I was on night patrol, he would come hang out at the big rock in the woods where the trails intersected. We spent more time surveilling each other than the woods and cabins around us.

At the end of each night we'd walk the perimeter, we

would check each cabin and return to the big rock in the woods where the trails intersected. He would gently bow down and kiss the back of my hand. Then cue the Clooney eyes and "Night, night, Heather bear. Sweet dreams."

On the nights we both had off, we'd find secretive places. Sometimes we'd just chat. Most of the time we'd do some sort of combo chatting and fooling around. Admittedly, the sex itself wasn't great. But I convinced myself that I was falling in love and that it was good enough.

That first summer I was always in the mood. The few times I wasn't, just one small shake of the head and he would immediately stop. There was no coercion. No pressure. No meant no. He was one of the good guys.

At one point the topic of feminism and the portrayal of female bodies in media came up. It was during a group conversation. I was taking a pretty staunch feminist position, emboldened by my years of bulimia and anorexia that had been influenced by those images. He pulled out a copy of *Maxim* magazine. It's not *Penthouse* or *Playboy*, but it's certainly more similar to those magazines than to *GQ* or *Esquire*. He justified his annual subscription. He said he could be a feminist and read these magazines. He said it isn't a big deal.

I protested and said that I wouldn't want any of my future daughters to see those pictures and feel the subtle pressure to match them. I told him I thought they sexually objectified women.

He said, "Oh c'mon. You're not one of *those* women, are

you? The ones who take everything too seriously? It isn't a big deal."

I shrugged and eventually stopped talking. I didn't want to be one of those women.

Thirty-Two Years

They were here! The English grandparents had arrived! His parents were pulling into the driveway and walking up our front stairs. As usual, they came with gifts.

My one-year-old daughter got new clothes and toddler treats.

My four-year-old son got a superhero magazine and a Thomas the Tank annual.

I got a new shirt and a home decorating magazine.

He got English sweets and a few Maxim magazines.

I rolled my eyes and sighed.

The stepdad said, "We've decided. This is the last time we're bringing those over. Clearly Heather doesn't like them and we're just going to bring you other stuff."

My husband good-naturedly said, "I'll just have to read these ones cover to cover and on repeat, then."

It'd been a decade of him receiving these magazines. A decade of me saying I found them disrespectful. A decade of him saying I'm overreacting. Two years of me saying I don't want those magazines in the house where the kids might see them. One year of me asking what he'll tell his daughter when she sees him ogling those barely clothed women who clearly had been photoshopped and probably ate far too little.

I think those magazines are disgraceful to both men and

women. They send a poor message to women and a dangerous message to men. They are a part of rape culture. Everyone is entitled to their own opinions. What you are not entitled to do is to put me down or disregard my beliefs or minimize my thoughts and feelings.

And yet, with just this one magazine, my husband had spent ten years doing just that.

And it wasn't him that ended it.

No, for a year after his supply ended, he'd laugh and say, "I would be reading my magazines right now if you hadn't convinced my parents to stop sending them." Chortle. Chortle. Isn't he funny.

Six Years

My dad found me crying on the bed. I told him I felt fat. He told me it was just baby fat and that it'll go away as I grow.

Ten Years

"Sit down, you fat cow!"

Before the boy on the bus could say anything more, I dropped my (apparently) fat ass down on the seat and my eyes down to the ground.

Eleven Years

"Have you lost weight?! You look fantastic!"

I didn't have an answer for my best friend's sister. I hadn't tried to lose weight. I didn't know I didn't look fantastic before. What I know now is that I'd gained the typical 5th grade pudge to gather up the stores of fat and tissue my body needed before entering puberty and growing taller and more womanly. What I learned then is that less weight equals more fantastic.

Twelve Years

I stood next to my dad at the dingy booth of the roadside café. He slapped my butt gently and said, "looks like Heather's rounding out! We're gonna need to watch what you eat."

Thirteen Years

"This is a really cute dress! You both should try it on."

"I'm not sure if my hips are small enough to look good in this."

"C'mon, Heather, let's do it. And besides, my mom's offering to buy them!"

My best friend and her mother convinced me to try on the dress. She and I came out of the side-by-side dressing rooms simultaneously. She looked super cute. She looked at me and said, "You do have big hips."

All the Years

Magazine covers. *Teen beat* and *Cosmopolitan* and all the headlines about how to lose weight, how to win the attention of your crush, how to give good head, how to transform yourself into something you aren't because nobody will like you as you are. Be skinnier. Be sexier. Don't be a slut. Don't be a prude. Wear form fitting clothes. Don't wear form fitting clothes unless you have the impossibly manufactured body of a model. Don't eat this. Do eat that. Just kidding, just don't eat.

Seventeen Years

At twelve I'd started dieting. My family stressors and an insecure body image, made an eating disorder of control and perfection bound to happen. As I had been identified as gifted as a young girl, I was already at higher risk of developing an eating disorder. Intelligence is a risk factor for them.

Now I was driving. Now I was able to access any food I wanted anytime I wanted. Now I was able to buy laxatives and tell my parents I'd eaten out. Now I was able to escape my family drama by numbing out to food and purging the food through overexercise and laxative abuse.

I wasn't worried though. I knew it was behavior I needed to hide and I knew what I was doing was a form of disordered eating, but in health class they always talked about self-induced vomiting and starving one's self. That's what a real eating disorder was. That's when I'd have to worry. If I got to the point of throwing up multiple times a day or eating no food, then I'd get help.

Eighteen Years

I ate one meal a day. I cried at the thought of eating more than that. My boyfriend begged me to eat more. The thought made me want to throw up. The hollow feeling in my stomach made me feel powerful. I'd try to hide the grumbling in my stomach so others wouldn't comment. I loved my little secret. I loved being able to feel hungry and deceive people into thinking I wasn't. I loved the control I had over myself. The less I ate, the weaker my body became, the stronger I felt.

I went to the gym daily and weighed myself before and after workouts. I got down to 120 pounds—five to 44 pounds underweight depending on the chart. But I wanted to get to 110. I felt like a failure, like I couldn't even starve myself effectively. My spirit felt as hollow as my stomach. I salivated over the food I saw around me but criticized every millimeter of my body. My hips were too big. I could pinch skin on my stomach. There wasn't a big enough gap between my thighs. My hip bones didn't jut out enough and my ribs were visible, but the skin wasn't yet tight over them. I needed to lose more.

My boyfriend knew. My best friend guessed. My parents didn't say anything. My brother made one comment about my really skinny legs, but I brushed it off. People commented on how small I'd gotten and how good I'd looked.

I don't know how it happened, but once I moved away to college my disorder morphed. I was eating more, but I was also binging and purging. Several nights a week I'd drive from my dorm to the nearby 24-hour Walmart. I'd load my cart with sweets and salty foods, usually in a dissociated daze. I'd numbly pay for it all, praying that no one I knew would see my full cart. I'd drive back to my dorm and watch myself devour all of it. Whole boxes of snack cakes, bags of chips, chocolates, cheese, boxes of cereal—everything in my cart would be gone within an hour. I felt nothing but urgency and numbness. Part of me wanted to stop. Part of me shamed myself. But those parts were standing outside of me, across the room, and weren't able to communicate with my body.

Uncomfortable, bloated, and ashamed, I'd swallow multiple laxatives, drink a glass of water, and wait for the food to be flushed out of me amid stomach cramps and endless diarrhea.

Eighteen Years
"Hey Heather! They were giving away free t-shirts at the student union. I wasn't sure what size you were so I just grabbed an XL."

My thoughtful friend meant no harm.

My brain heard "See. She thinks you're fat too."

Nineteen years
"It's nice to meet you," I said to my brother's future mother-in-law and his two future sisters-in-law.

Just us girls. My mom, my future sister-in-law, her mom and sisters, and myself all crowded into a small bridal shop somewhere in southern Minnesota. The hunt for the bridesmaid dresses had begun.

It was meant to be fun. Dress shopping with the girls. I hated trying on clothes in front of anyone ever. I'm not very fashion or makeup conscious, and the proposal, "let's-do-our-nails-and-hair-together" has never filled me with joy. Also, I was only a couple months out of therapy and away from my binging and purging. I still didn't like my body and the thought of coming out of a dressing room in front of skinny women I didn't really know, so that they could judge how good I looked in a particular dress did not sound awesome.

But there I was. The nice girl who was trained not to say no and who didn't raise her voice.

We tried on one dress. It was ok.

The store didn't have the second dress in all our sizes.

Third dress was an empire waist which I loved and was comfortable in. No one else liked it.

So we came to the fourth dress. I didn't want to try it on in the first place. But I didn't want to be a bitch, so off into the dressing room I went.

I didn't want to come out, but out I went.

The oohs and awws abounded. "Imagine them all holding candles walking down the aisles. It'd be gorgeous!"

The dresses were solid sequins. The candle-light would flicker and reflect off my abdomen. They weren't just solid sequins, though. They were skin tight and literally showed every curve, bump, and angle of our bodies.

I stood there pulling at the one I wore, sucking in my stomach, pretending to be somewhere else until we could try on the next dress.

They talked more and more about it. They were falling in love with it. They were going to choose this dress. I wanted to cry. But I wasn't going to say no. Good girls don't say no or make themselves inconvenient.

I tried taking deep breaths while sucking in my stomach (not easy) and felt the tears puddling behind my lower lids.

I was hiding it sufficiently until I heard my future sister-in-law's mom laugh, "We're going to have Heather and my daughter doing sit ups until the wedding!"

I ducked back into the dressing room and the tears broke the levy of my eyelids. I took so long getting myself recombobulated that my mom eventually knocked on the door. I told her I wouldn't be comfortable in that dress. We left, and I cried the entire drive home with my mom reassuring me that she wouldn't let that dress be picked. It wasn't. Instead, she made all the bridesmaids dresses. I bought more laxatives.

Twenty-Two Years
My Prince Charming wanted to know everything about me. He wanted to know the good, the bad, the ugly. The hurts and heroics. The prides and the shames.

I explained to him that I was a year into recovery from an eating disorder. I told him I still wasn't comfortable with my appearance. I told him that I can't handle anyone talking about what I'm eating. I told him that I was generally past the behaviors, but that my mind hadn't caught up yet.

He hugged me and said he'd support me. He said that I was beautiful.

I melted.

We went to a thrift store. He told me to try on some form fitting shirts and pants that hugged my butt. I told him I wouldn't feel comfortable.

He encouraged me.

I tried them on and he gushed over how amazing I looked.

I bought three shirts and two pairs of pants.

He helped me feel more comfortable about my body.

The camp director mentioned that the peanut butter had been decreasing more rapidly than expected and asked who was making PB and fluff sandwiches.

My handsome knight in shining camp attire said, "Actually that's been me. I noticed a few girls who haven't been eating much for meals, so I started a pb club. We go down to the kitchen every night and make malts and pb & fluff sandwiches. I figured they seem like they might be struggling with eating disorders and this could be a way to get them to eat. Then we have some good conversations while we're at it."

Swoon. This man cared about girls' wellness. He noticed eating disorders and found ways to be understanding and still keep them safe. He gets it.

He also got a crowd of six teenage girls ogling him every night, but no one seemed to consider that.

Twenty-Three Years
"Hey. Thanks for grocery shopping. I thought I'd asked for _____ (fill in the blank)."

"You did? I don't remember that."

"Yep. Look, it's written right here on the list."

"Oh, I guess I forgot."

"Oh. Well, you probably don't need to eat as much of that anyway."

"Heather, are those pants a little tight on you? You look great, I just wasn't sure if they're comfortable."

"Heather, I know we don't have a lot of money, but we can get you clothes that fit if those are getting too small. Just trying to help."

"Heather, is that your second bowl of cereal?"

Twenty-Five Years

"Can you please stop talking about what I eat?"

"I was only joking, lighten up."

There was an odd laugh he had. It's hard to describe, but it was distinct and communicated his point loud and clear.

Laughter is meant to be light, fun, loving. It is meant to evoke feelings of warmth and joy. Laughter is meant to be shared and delightful.

His laughter was different. Instead of being light, fun and loving it was dark, heavy and dripping with disdain. Rather than evoking pleasant feelings, I was left with shame, inferiority and isolated quiet.

His laughter should be called something different. In fact, in an effort to discover a suitable replacement word, I looked "laughter" up in a thesaurus. Under "antonyms for laughter" were just four words: sadness, unhappiness, despair, gloom. *His* laughter was the antonym for laughter. He anti-laughs.

And yet while I was living with it, I thought it was laughter. Something felt off about it and I felt sadness, unhappiness, despair and gloom in response to it, but it *sounded* like laughter. He *said* he was joking. Maybe I *was* too sensitive and needed to lighten up.

"Can you please stop talking about what I eat?"

"I was only joking, lighten up." Anti-laugh.

"I know that you didn't know me when I was really active in my eating disorder, so I get that you may need reminders, but I *really* can't tolerate anyone commenting on my food. The eating disorder voice is hard not to listen to. It tells me that everyone is watching what I eat. That I shouldn't eat this or that. That I'm ugly and fat and unacceptable. *Any* comment about what I'm eating only reaffirms the eating disorder. I've asked you before, please don't comment about food."

"Right. I forgot. I won't."

It seemed supportive. It seemed he listened. He said all the right things. But he spoke flatly and walked out of the room.

Twenty-Eight Years

I was seven months into carrying our first child when he started calling me "House."

"Oh my god! Look at your belly! You're huge!" Anti-laugh.

I must have looked crestfallen because he quickly said, "But you're supposed to be. You're growing our kid. Your big belly is the house for our little guy. House! You're a house!" More anti-laughter.

"What did you just call me?" I fake laughed. I couldn't show him it was upsetting. He was just joking after all.

"House! I don't mean you're fat. I meant you're currently our baby's house."

"Uhh. Okay. But, could I be a condo or something instead? Something a little smaller sounding?"

For years he'd joke to people that he called me house while I was pregnant. His audience would look at me to determine what response would be appropriate. I'd smile and say it was fine, I knew he was joking. Pretend laugh.

Thirty-Four Years

"Is it seriously gone already?! I just bought that a couple days ago! How could you possibly have eaten all of it in just a couple days!"

"Hey. Again, could you please stop commenting about what I eat or don't eat. It's been over a decade. I'm not sure why it's hard for you to remember that any comments about my food feel like judgment to me."

"Right. I know. I wasn't judging. It's just impressive that you could eat all that in such a quick time!"

Thirty-Six Years

"I'm so glad I bought you that treadmill. It's so easy to move and not a waste of money at all," seething sarcasm.

"Well I'm not the only one that could be using it," I said.

"But I bought it for *you*. And how many times have you used it?"

"I mean, I've been pregnant and recovering from childbirth, and starting a business while working full time, breastfeeding and being mommy to three young kids. Not to mention I've been a little stressed and down since my dad died, my grandma died, my mom's home was burglarized, and my mom's been diagnosed with breast cancer—all in the last 9 months."

"Whatever. I just shouldn't have ever bought it. Fucking waste of money and space."

"I'll use it. I just need to get some energy back. Grief and a newborn are exhausting."

"Whatever."

Thirty-Eight Years

"Hey, Bear. I've been so proud of you and all the work you've been doing trying to lose weight. You deserve a little treat."

He gently tossed a giant sized Reese's bar and a Symphony bar at me.

"Uhh. . . . thanks?"

"You just deserve to have a little cheat day."

"I just . . . I'm not sure what to say . . ."

"Don't you want it?!"

"Of course I do, but I also don't want it, because I don't want to go backwards and eating less chocolate has been really hard for me."

"Fine! I was just trying to do something nice. That's what I get for trying to be supportive and kind. I won't ever do anything nice for you again. I'm so sorry." The sarcasm seeped across the room and grabbed me around the throat. The disdain grabbed what was left of my weary soul and held it down. My mind told me I was being ungrateful. Of course, he was just being nice and one candy bar wouldn't be a problem.

"No. No. I didn't mean to sound ungrateful. It was very sweet of you. Thank you."

I ate the candy bars.

One month later, as I was eating a candy bar, he walked into a room, sneered and said, "I thought you were trying to cut back on the chocolate?"

Forty Years

"Dad, can I have a mom special?"

"What?"

My daughter responded, "Mom, tell him what I mean."

Without taking my eyes off my book I shouted from the chair just outside the kitchen, "It's a mug with mixed milk chocolate and white chocolate chips."

"Yeah," said my daughter, "you put them in layers and then mix it all together. It's soooo good."

"Why is it called the mom special?" my husband asked.

"A couple weeks ago I came downstairs and saw mom making her own cup of mixed chocolate chips, so I call it the mom special."

"Well of course she'd do something like that. She'll find sugar anywhere. It's perfect that it's called the mom special."

Later that night I reminded him, for yet another time in our nearly twenty years together, to please make no comments about my food.

Forty-One Years

"Did you really eat the last of the provolone?"

I didn't know how to answer. There wouldn't be a good answer anyway. The sneer, the tone, made it clear I'd disappointed or done something wrong.

"I bought that for our son. I bet he didn't even get any of it because you always eat it all."

For a moment, I wanted to respond with rational irritation. "It's just fucking cheese."

But my gut hollered that I should be ashamed. I eat too much. I have no self-control. I'm selfish and put my own desires in front of my son. I was wrong and a disappointment.

Forty Years

We're all laughing, really laughing. We're enjoying time together. I've always said my husband and I are best around other people. We have fun; we don't argue. I feel loved and desired. When other people are around.

But everything shifts quickly. I make a joke or comment that he doesn't like. There is a subtle shift in the color of his eyes, and a sudden flash of anger that disappears as quickly as it arrived. He straightens his shoulders and tilts his chin.

A few minutes later, he laughs and repeats the story of the "mom special" incident. It is unmistakably the anti-laugh. He is ridiculing me for eating chocolate chips.

My own fake laughter hides my shame. I'm sure no one else thinks anything of it.

Part of me gave him the benefit of the doubt. He'd

forgotten again. But really, both he and I knew what he was doing. The malice had been too obvious to completely ignore. He put me in my place and I watched my words for the rest of the night.

Still, I didn't totally surrender. AGAIN, I asked him not to talk about what I ate, and especially not in front of other people.

"It's our friends!" he replied, exasperated. "They don't care."

It was true. They wouldn't have cared. That was enough to persuade me that I was overreacting once again. I swallowed and denied my own feelings.

No, our friends wouldn't have cared, But I did. I just didn't realize that this alone should have been enough.

Forty-Four Years

I open the fridge to grab a quick snack. I grab the provolone cheese and check to make sure I'm not taking the last of it. My gut feels heavy and twisted. I ask myself whether I should take a slice at all.

It's just fucking cheese.

Twenty-Two Years

He wrote me a poem.

He wrote me a poem!

I was enamored.

It was the first makeshift talent show of the summer, after we'd been "dating" for almost two weeks. I never knew what to call it, because you can't "date" at camp. You live together 24/7. I used to proclaim that this explained our relationship. It didn't *really* move quickly when you considered that we were together 24/7 and saw the good parts and not so good parts of each other under the stress and joy of camp.

Almost two weeks of romancing with the Englishman and he gets up in front of the crowd of campers. He glances at me, licks his lips and begins.

The kid campers oohed and he sweetly looked at me. My counselor friends subtly nudged me. He wrote me a poem. And not only did he write me a poem, but he proclaimed it in front of a room full of people.

Be still my heart.

Forty-One Years
"Hey. I know you're staying at the hotel to write and produce content and stuff. Do you think you'd want a little break?"

"What did you have in mind?"

"I mean, I don't want to be presumptive, but hotel sex is kinda hot."

I agreed and told him to come after the younger two are in bed and our oldest can watch them. I was literally staying in the same town where we lived.

I did this fairly often. In fact, I did this quarterly. It was the best way for me to be able to focus and get into the flow. I couldn't do that with kids, dogs and home life interrupting me every five minutes.

The first time I went away on my own was for a mental break. I take on the brunt of the care of our autistic daughter.

I get the worst of the behaviors and meltdowns. I schedule the tests and therapies, read the books, and do the advocating. A University of WI-Madison study showed that moms of autistic children have the same levels of stress chemicals coursing through their bodies as people in combat do. So, yeah, I needed a break.

I am an introvert. A break for me means no one around. It takes me 15 minutes or more to gear up for a phone conversation with my favorite people. I'd be quite happy not encountering another human for weeks, maybe months.

You can imagine my excitement at a weekend alone. Two nights. Two days. No one to answer to. No chores to complete. Just me and myself and books and HGTV and hiking and a bed for napping. Bliss.

At about 6 o'clock on my first night there, he called.

"Hey. What room are you in?"

"<insert room number here> Why?"

"No reason." Click

Two minutes later there's a knock at my door. I look through the peephole and I see him. Grinning like it's an amazing surprise.

I open the door and try to appear pleased.

"Oh, hi," I say. "What are you doing here? Where are the kids?"

"Surprise! I got your mom to watch them for a few hours. I've been planning this for a week and couldn't wait to surprise you. I figured we could get dinner, have a date, fool around and then I'll leave you to yourself."

I felt like crying. Not tears of happiness but tears of disappointment. This was not what I'd wanted. I didn't want to see people. I'd been seeing people for weeks on end without a break. And yet, here in front of me was a person, who apparently thought he was being kind, but who was, in reality, raining on my solitary parade.

"Oh," I say. "Well, I just took a shower and got into my pjs. I was going to order a pizza and just watch tv."

"OK!" he enthusiastically replied. "We don't have to go out!"

I couldn't help it. A sigh slipped out.

"You don't seem happy to see me. I'm sorry. I've ruined everything. I just thought we don't get time to see each other alone very much and I thought it'd be great to connect with you. But I get it if you don't want me around. I'll just leave." Sad, dejected head tipped down.

"No. No," I acquiesce. "Don't leave. It's just not what I was expecting, you know? Like that initial disappointment when things aren't going the way you thought they would? But, yeah, it'll be fun. Take off your shoes, cuddle up in the bed, and let's order pizza."

Still not what I wanted.

I smiled as we ate. I smiled when he said something nice. I smiled when he changed the channel to something "we both wanted to watch" (which, as always, was what he wanted to watch and I tolerated). I said "sure" when he noticed the time and said that if we were going to have sex, we should probably do that soon before he had to get back to the kids. I smiled and said goodbye as he immediately pulled his pants back on, grabbed his keys, said goodnight and headed out the door.

That was my first weekend "alone."

This time was different. This time we had agreed that I'd be working. I'd agreed ahead of time for him to come over.

I anticipated a bottle of wine. Or flowers. Or a smile.

Instead, he showed up with nothing and started kissing me. By this point I didn't like kissing him, so I moved my face away and directed him toward my neck.

We did the deed.

He said, "That was fun. Love you. Don't want to keep you from your work."

He got dressed.

He left.

I was a booty call.

The next time I was in a local hotel and he suggested he come by, I said, "That's fine, but can it be a bit more than a booty call. I felt really used last time."

He said, "What does that mean?"

"I don't know. Some type of romance or something. Poems or music or something to help me feel connected to you."

The man who twenty years earlier had read me my poem in front of a full room and kissed my hand every night and danced with me in the parking lot needed me to tell him explicitly how to be romantic.

He showed up with an old book of poetry.

He flipped a few pages in and read a poem.

It felt gross and forced and not what I needed.

We got into an argument.

He said I wasn't clear and I just needed to tell him what I wanted. We'd been married for nearly two decades and we'd had this conversation a million and one times. We have had all the talks. This wasn't a situation in which I was expecting him to read my mind. It was a situation in which I was expecting him to remember who I am, what I like, how I feel loved.

I said, "Honestly? All you would have had to do was come in, look me in the eyes and recite my poem."

He said it.

He yawned, said he was tired but that if I wanted him to stay, he would. He was worried he'd fall asleep, though.

He left.

Twenty-Seven Years

"The professor of my couples therapy class made an interesting point. She said that men have sex to get close and women get close to have sex. What do you think about that?"

My spouse barely glanced up from his video game before saying, "yeah, I guess that makes sense."

"So, you know, let's maybe make sure we do things to feel more connected before just going at it at night?"

"Yeah. Okay."

Thirty-Eight Years

I'd been trying to figure out how to have a more fulfilling sex life. We'd go for a little bit having sex a couple times a week and then it'd be months. I was dissatisfied. He was dissatisfied.

We spent our days separately. One of us worked outside of the home while the other worked inside the home with our three children. We met up at night and on the weekends. There was very little time for the two of us to connect. We'd problem solved and it typically ended with me saying, "Remember, men have sex to get close and women get close to have sex." He'd agree. I'd say I needed more connection. I needed to play table top games together or have conversations or even watch a movie together. Anything together.

He'd say, "Yeah. You're right. I'll be more intentional about that."

Nothing would change.

A day or two later he'd turn to me and say "Wanna have sex?"

Nothing had changed, but I'd either acquiesce and then feel used or say no and then he'd say "fine" and roll away with his back to me.

I wanted it to change.

After the most recent problem-solving round, he turned to me and said, "Wanna have sex?"

I said, "Not really. Nothing's changed. We haven't connected at all and I need to feel connected. But we could talk or something and maybe I'd get there?"

His response? He grumbled something, rolled over and made his disappointment clearly known.

I said, "So that's it? I am not ready to be fucked, but

asked for connection to help me feel like I wanted to have sex with you and you just turn away?"

With his body still positioned away from me he turned his head back a quarter of a turn, looked at me with uncaring eyes and said, "It's 10 o'clock at night, I'm too tired to talk in the hopes that you might feel like doing it."

And he turned his head back to his tablet.

I'd straightforwardly asked for connection and he refused. Men have sex to get close, I reasoned, so maybe he's just feeling disconnected too. I could be the bigger person, the good woman who puts others before herself and make sure my husband felt cared for. I could set aside my needs to give him what he needs. As his needs are filled, he'll naturally have more energy to give me what I need.

I decided I'd have sex with him every night for a week.

I talked myself up to it.

I put aside any previous feelings of rejection.

I met him at the door with a kiss, took my clothes off and pressed my bare breasts against his back, touched him. Three nights I did this to get the spark back. Three nights, whether I really wanted to or not, I tried to fill my husband's needs and be the good wife.

The fourth night, I started in again.

He said with a smile, "What's gotten into you, lately?"

I said, "I've just decided to give you sex every night for a week." (Side note: "Give him sex" is one of the worst phrases ever created. It is part of rape culture. It presumes that all men want sex all the time while women don't. It presumes that sex is a gift that we give to them and that we're obligated to let the man have his way. Women like sex too. Women aren't the keepers of the sex and men aren't the takers. It's meant to be mutual.)

He said, "Oh. OK. But maybe we can skip it tonight. I'm kinda tired."

We skipped it.

This went on for a couple more nights. Nothing else had changed. No hugs during the day. No nice texts or compliments or quality time. Nothing changed. Except at night I'd make a move and he'd either go for it or not.

After a while I stopped.

One night he made a move. I said no. He rolled over in a huff and said I'm never in the mood.

Later that year, still desperate to figure things out and improve our sex life, I came upon a podcast. The interviewee claimed women need to feel safe in bed before they'll feel completely open to sexual connection. She suggested scheduling time weekly in which the woman is completely in charge. No interruptions allowed. Locked bedroom door. Husband and wife together on the bed. Wife directs everything and husband goes along with it. Husband's goal is to help the wife feel safe. Wife's goal is to feel comfortable and in control of the sex life. Husband gets no commentary, though obviously he can say no if there's something he isn't comfortable doing.

I suggested this to him. He said, "sure."

I said, "So remember, it's all about space for me to direct things. It doesn't necessarily mean we'll have sex."

"Yep," he said.

We scheduled it. Told our kids to leave us alone for 30 minutes and gave them their devices. Locked the door. I told him to lie down and I placed my head on his chest. I told him to hug me tighter. He did. Just when I was starting to feel more relaxed and connected, he said, "Is this it?" I reinforced the point of the exercise and that, yes, I was feeling connected and this time was for me. He said, "Yeah, yeah, I get it. You're right. Sorry."

Second time. Kids with devices, door locked, I lie down on him and ask him to kiss my neck. No sex. Just making out.

Third time. Kids. Devices. Door. Lie down. I'm lying on him. He starts to move and touch my nipple. I stop him and say, "Hey—I'm in control!" with a coy smile. He stops. We lie quietly a little longer. I begin to make conversation. He reaches for my nipple. I again tell him I'm in control; it's my time and it can look whatever way I want it to. He said, "Seriously? Is this what it's going to be? Just lying here cuddling and talking? I thought this was about sex." I reminded him of the purpose and the guidelines. He said, "I don't want to just lie here for nothing to come from it. I agreed to this because it was supposed to lead to sex."

I cried and got out of bed. We never tried it again.

Twenty-Two Years

"You brought a Hugo Boss suit to work at a summer camp?" I laughed.

He hung his head bashfully and nodded with a smile.

That was him. Fashion conscious, sophisticated, witty, European. He charmed and wooed and it worked, but it didn't match up to my sense of who a camp counselor would be. His friend, the curly haired hippy with the kind eyes and smile who slept above the arthouse and smelled like he hadn't showered for a few weeks, epitomized my idea of a camp counselor. The dude with an English accent and long strutting walk, who shared stories of working as a bouncer at a nightclub and brought his Hugo Boss suit and dress boots, did not.

So, I asked him, "Why did you want to work at a summer camp? You don't seem like you're into the great outdoors or camp-like activities."

He said, "It was a cheap way to travel around the states. I've always wanted to come back to the states since I went to Florida when I was twelve. Plus, I like new things and I'm not *against* the outdoors."

"What about you?" he asked. "Why did you come out to Maine to be a camp counselor?"

"I love being outside and being with kids. My favorite things to do are hike and backpack."

"Oh yeah? Hiking is just taking a walk. I like taking walks. Never been backpacking before."

"I love it. The most free and relaxed I've ever felt is when I've been backpacking. I plan to thru-hike the Appalachian Trail someday."

"What's that mean?"

"It's hiking from Georgia to Maine and takes from three to six months, depending on how fast you hike."

"That sounds really cool. I'll do that with you."

"But you don't really like hikes and you've never been backpacking? That's a long trip to take to figure out whether you like it or not."

"Yeah, but I like a good challenge."

The year before we got married, he talked about the Appalachian Trail with me. He planned and dreamed. It appeared my dream was becoming his. I couldn't believe how amazing he was. This handsome, debonair English man with a cute little dimple, who loved kids and cared about girls with eating disorders, was romantic and sweet AND he was growing to love the outdoors as much as I did.

Twenty-Four Years

We'd moved to Colorado. Opportunities to hike and backpack surrounded us. We went on a hike close to home. He complained about the heat the entire time.

We went on a hike a little further away. He complained about walking back and forth across the side of the mountain. I explained switchbacks and why they're helpful to avoid a steep uphill climb. He continued to complain.

We went on a third hike together. He was relaxed and cheerful and told me how much he liked hiking with me. I knew he was seeing the light and becoming an outdoor man.

We went on a hike higher up in the mountains. He complained about how straight up it was and wanted to know where the switchbacks were. He cheered up a little when we got to the top and the high mountain prairie opened up ahead of us. This mood shifted quickly when he attempted to jump over a small creek and landed with one foot in the water. He complained that his foot was wet and cold. I gave him a blowjob to cheer him up. I told him it was only a little further to get to a mountaintop peak. He said he didn't want to go and he'd be worried if I went alone, but that I could go if I wanted. We headed back down.

I started hiking alone. It was far more enjoyable without the continual complaining.

I mentioned the Appalachian Trail. He said he still wanted to go. I said you complain every time we hike. He said it isn't all the time.

We went on a hike together. It was a hike I'd taken before and loved. It had a stretch of bouldering and ended with a beautiful overlook of the Colorado River miles below. He lost his footing on the bouldering, fell, slipped a few yards and scratched his leg. I said we could turn around. He said, no, he'd be fine and didn't want to ruin it for me. We continued. He complained the entire way.

Thirty-Two Years

"Depending on the personalities of our kids, I think we could still do the Appalachian Trail in five or six years."

"There's no way a child would hike that long."

"If we start them hiking now and make the hikes progressively longer, it'll just be what they're used to. Obviously, we need to see what our daughter's temperament is like, but I think our son could do it."

"You're more than welcome to take them hiking" he replied disinterestedly while flipping through the channels.

"We'd probably want to do some overnight camping."

"Yeah. Sure. You get it all arranged and I'll go with you. Not until they are past the toddler age, though. It sounds like a lot of work to constantly try to keep them out of the fire."

Thirty-Seven Years

"I'm thinking I'd like to get myself in hiking shape and do a longer trail across the north shore."

"Oh yeah? How long would that take?"

"It's about three weeks."

"You can't leave the kids for three weeks. Not to mention you're definitely not in shape to do three straight weeks of hiking."

"I could plan it out and each kid could come join me for a portion of the trip. Like maybe four days at a time. I could start with our oldest. Then, after a few days, you could come up with our daughter and bring him back. A few days more and we could swap out for the little guy."

"Are you kidding me? That's a lot of back and forth for me. But, whatever. If that's what you want to do, then I guess you'll figure out a way that isn't too much work for me or the kids."

I stopped planning it.

His words implied that he'd support me; that he'd do whatever it took to help me accomplish my goal. But I knew that tone. He might move through the motions, but there'd be strings attached. He'd complain the entire time while subtly asserting I was selfish for putting him out so immensely. He'd mention how much the kids missed me and that I wasn't being fair to them. He'd leave the home a mess and say he was doing the best he could, given he was solo parenting for three weeks. He'd begrudge me my peace.

Twenty-Two Years

"What are you doing?" he asked.

"My head hurts so bad, I figured that maybe if I curled up in a small enough ball, I'd be too small for the headache and it'd have to leave," I whispered.

I had a migraine. A horrible, nausea-creating, pixelated vision, sensitivity to light and sound migraine. It was not the first and it would not be the last.

"Oh my sweet Heather Bear." He gently grabbed me closer and stroked my back. He closed the blinds, turned off the lights, asked my roommates to be quieter and came back to lay near me. He told me a gentle story with a quiet voice until I fell asleep.

Twenty-Three Years

"I'm getting a little scared. I've had the weird vision thing that usually leads into a migraine for three hours now. The aura usually only lasts thirty minutes and then the pain sets in. I don't feel any pain, but my vision is messed up."

He reassured me, told me to lay down and that he'd be home as soon as he could catch the next bus. He held my hand as he drove me to the emergency room. He asked the doctors and nurses to speak quietly and dim the lights. I felt cared for.

We learned it was just another type of migraine and headed home. He tucked me into bed, closed the door and let me sleep it off.

Twenty-Five Years

Colorado was awesome, but adjusting to the altitude took me weeks. I was short of breath, had difficulty sleeping and developed allergies. It wasn't fun. However, those first few weeks were nothing compared to the following fall.

Six weeks of migraine. Six straight weeks of headache and nausea, sound and light sensitivity, pain and vomiting. Six weeks of language impairment as I tried to eloquently ask professors for extensions and makeup work for the classes I missed.

During the first ER trip I threw up in the car. Thankfully we'd brought a bucket. My husband sweetly tutted and expressed sympathy. He helped me to the ER, checked me in while I was in the bathroom throwing up again, and sat by my side as I vomited all over the ER floor and waited for the IV drugs to take me to a place where I no longer vomited or felt pain.

On the second ER trip he sighed and said, "Do you really have to go? It can't be that bad again. They're going to think you're a drug seeker." He walked me to the car, checked me in while I was vomiting in the bathroom, and sat by my side—but without gentleness or care. I apologized for putting him out. I was lying in a hospital bed, IVs in my arm, lights out, eyes closed, and I apologized for putting him out. He sighed and said it was fine. His tone said it was not.

On the way to the ER for the third time he said, "You've really got to figure this out. I can't keep doing this. Can you at least decide earlier in the day if you have to go to the ER? These late-night trips interfere with my sleep and then I have a hard time at work the next day."

I did have to go to the ER again. And I felt anxious about asking my own husband if he could drive me.

Twenty-Seven Years

I came home from work with a migraine. I was lucky that I'd caught it early so I could drive myself home. I dreaded asking him to come pick me up. There was no easy way to get me and the car home without a lot of coordinating and back and forth trips. I understood why he'd get annoyed if I was unsafe to drive.

But this time I caught it early and drove myself home. I walked through the door to find the empty apartment I expected, and slunk my way to the bed to try to sleep the migraine away.

I was still in my scrubs, laying on the bed, when he came home. He asked how I had beaten him home. I told him I left early. As I was about to explain why, he cut me off and said, "I know. I know. You have a migraine." I felt shamed, broken, an inconvenience.

"I watched my grandad take care of my grandmother for decades," he said. "Even before the MS she was sickly and he always took care of her. I'm not going to do that. I'm not going to get stuck being the one to take care of you while you're always sick. It's getting old."

"Imagine what it's like to be the one who's actually in pain and getting the migraines," I whispered.

"I'm sure it sucks, but this isn't all about you. This affects both of us and I'm not just going to put up with constant complaining and sickness."

It stung. I felt alone and unloved. I internally vowed to be less sick, less selfish, and to suck it up and deal with it.

Thirty-Seven Years

I was home with the flu. It was hard to get out of bed to go to the bathroom. Everything ached, and I was fairly certain death would have been preferable.

That first day I came home with a fever, my spouse felt my head and my stomach, sighed, and told me to go into the bedroom and lock the door. He'd take care of the kids and I should sleep.

He'd occasionally come in and ask me if I needed anything. Each time he did he seemed more and more frazzled, less and less interested in actually getting me anything I'd need.

One time he came in and asked and, as I was about to ask for some applesauce, he sighed and looked put out. I told him I'd rather he not ask if he was going to be moody about it. He said of course he's moody; he's taking care of three children and a sick wife and he's tired. There was no care. No compassion. His words and body language conveyed his annoyance and disdain. I told him I was fine and didn't need anything. No way I would be more of an inconvenience than I already was.

That night he asked me to sleep downstairs in the guest room because my coughing was annoying and kept him up. He then backtracked and tried to persuade me that it'd be in my best interest to sleep on the less comfortable bed in the cold basement because the kids wouldn't wake me up in the middle of the night.

I went, but I knew it wasn't for me.

It wasn't the first time he'd asked me to sleep downstairs when I was sick. There had been times previously when he'd angrily say, "Would you please stop coughing!" When I called him on it, he'd (anti) laugh and say he was joking.

I'd thought about talking to him for a solid week. I considered how I wanted to approach him and how to explain the problem. I'd tried explaining the shame, the disdain, the feeling of being an inconvenience several times before. He never seemed to understand. He'd play victim and say he was tired too. He'd say he didn't mean to be snippy but he was stressed. Nothing would change.

This time I said, "I'd really like to talk to you about something."

Sigh. "Well that's never a start to a happy conversation."

"I've been trying to figure out how to explain what I need when I'm sick. You do a great job of taking care of me, but it's hard for me not to personalize your stress or tone while you're doing it. We're asked to serve joyfully, and I guess that's what I feel is missing. Compassion and joyful giving."

"You want me to be joyful when you're sick?"

"No. That's not it, but when you do things to take care of me, at least be kind instead of crabby."

"My god. I can't even help the right way. It's always something with you." And he walked out of the room.

Twenty -Two Years

Faith had always been an important part of my life. Some of my earliest memories were of me lying on my floor, praying and asking to understand concepts like the Trinity and the purpose of the crucifixion. I spent summers at a Christian Summer Camp where I felt my spiritual life grow and my faith become more personal. I left college expecting to pursue a cooperative MDiv/MSW to become an ordained minister and serve as a hospice chaplain. Faith was important to me.

By the time I applied to work at the Quaker camp, I had grown beyond the black and white Bible-thumping ideologies of my teen years. My faith broadened toward complexity and ambiguity. While I previously adored the seeming security of the black and white, I'd grown to appreciate and reside in the gray. Faith was still important to me, but I was not going to presume it needed to look a certain way or be important to anyone else.

In our early weeks of conversation I declared my faith and my openness to him. I explained the benefit and meaning I received from having a relationship with God. He explained that he never really attended church and it just wasn't important to him. I told him I believed that so long as someone is striving to find purpose and be the best human they can be, particular beliefs were inconsequential.

A couple of weeks after our first kiss he told me a story. One time he'd had a bad headache and someone had touched his head and prayed and the headache went away. That unexplained healing always stuck with him, he said, and it kept him from being completely atheistic. He defined himself as agnostic. My heart swelled and I knew that this was the opening God needed. I knew that his belief or disbelief would not factor into my decision to remain in relationship with him. After all, the Bible declares that faithful women should stay with and pray for their unbelieving husbands, and in so doing will bring their husbands to salvation.

A couple weeks after our first date we stood in the dewy soccer field beneath the glimmering stars and full moon. He kissed me. He said he loved me. I didn't respond. He kissed me again, passionately. Again, I didn't respond and said, "I just can't". He knew my recent betrayal. He knew the distrust

I felt after my boyfriend of four years broke up with me over a phone call in a common hallway. He responded with, "One more kiss."

I thought that if he tried to turn it sexual there would be no way I'd say I loved him. I thought that I wasn't ready. I thought that if I didn't say I loved him, he'd feel rejected and move on.

It was a sweet kiss, a kiss of the kind I'd seen in romantic movies. It was the kiss that convinced me to tell him I loved him too.

The next day, he found me before breakfast.

He asked how I was feeling and said, "Can I tell you something crazy and you won't judge me?"

"Of course," I said.

"Last night, when we were in the field. I was going to stop, but I heard someone tell me to kiss you one more time. It was so clear. I believe it was God telling me to kiss you once more. And because of that kiss you were able to say you love me too. I really think God wants us together. That we're supposed to be together."

I smiled and hugged him and told him I believe that, too.

After our summer at camp, he traveled with me to my new home in Milwaukee. I was beginning a full-time volunteer job at a neighborhood church. He was going to help me move before flying back to England to finish his final year of university.

We arrived to an empty house and a set alarm system. We quickly learned the system worked and that we had the incorrect code. When the lights flashed and the noise sounded, he shouted, "Jesus Christ!" After we got the alarm turned off and the call to the police canceled, I asked him to try not to say "Jesus Christ" in that way. You bet your ass I'm fine with spicing up some shitty language with fucking powerful four-letter prose. The one thing that bothers me, however, is shouting "Jesus Christ" as though he's a swear word. Of course he understood and promised to stop.

The following Sunday he, my roommates, and I were running late to church. We planned to worship at the church where I would be working. I was going to be introduced to the congregation that day and my job would begin the next.

We arrived late. As I walked in the side door, I saw the entire choir lined up in the entryway, waiting to enter the sanctuary singing the opening hymn. I heard the prelude playing and saw everyone other than the pastor and the choir sitting worshipfully in their seats. The pastor spotted me and was heading over to shake hands when I heard a loud Englishman shout with pain and rage, "Jesus Fucking Christ!" The prelude had simultaneously finished and his words seemed to echo through the old church building. The choir turned with curiosity and disapproval. I sheepishly shook hands with the pastor and said, "Hi, I'm Heather, these are my roommates and that tall guy in the back holding his head is my fiancé."

Thirty-Seven Years

Over the years, faith became a hot and cold topic. He'd refrain from using "Jesus Christ" as a swear word long enough for me to feel comfortable, only to allow it to slowly sneak back into his vocabulary. Every three to six months I'd remind him that I found it offensive and ask him to stop using it. He'd stop. Never an apology. Always just, "oh, yeah, I forgot."

In Denver, when I searched for a church, he told me to go ahead and maybe he'd come sometimes.

Just when I would worry that our values were too disparate and that perhaps a similar faith was more important than I initially thought, he'd talk about praying. He'd say that he prays daily for me. I'd say I hadn't thought he believed in God. He'd say, "I never said that."

As the deep conversations of our early courtship faded into distant memories, I'd buy spirituality books, or couples devotions, or suggest meditation or couples yoga. He'd play along and seem interested. My heart would feel hopeful and I'd know that God was working in mysterious ways.

There were times his anger seemed relentless and chronically simmering below the surface. I'd suggest he find some sort of spiritual practice. He'd agree that might help, purchase a book or two, but not read them.

I'd listen to Christian rock. He'd mock it and me. I'd confront him about that. He'd say he was only joking and remind me that it just wasn't his thing. Then he would share a story about how he felt God when he was outside playing with the kids.

I'd try to keep the actual meaning of Christmas front and center. On Christmas morning I wanted to read the Bible's account of the birth of Jesus before we began opening presents. He would wait until the kids were excited and ready to start opening their gifts and then, with a smirk he'd say, "Oh wait. That's right. Mom wants us to read the Bible first." It stung. The kids would roll their eyes, following their father's lead. I was the bad guy and Jesus was the stranger kid keeping them from enjoying the best part of Christmas.

This all culminated in one interesting turn of events. Our church's children's minister had resigned. They were looking for a volunteer to lead Vacation Bible School. They were also looking for a replacement employee.

I volunteered to lead VBS and remembered how much I loved this type of work. I mentioned this to my husband and he suggested I apply for the job. That seemed impractical as it meant adding a thirty-hour job to my already over-scheduled week. He said maybe we could job share it.

My jaw dropped.

"You'd want to work at the church?" I asked.

"Sure," he said. "It can't be that hard."

"You'd be leading youth group. You'd have to believe in and teach about God."

"Yeah, I know. I've been doing a lot of growing in that and I'm more spiritual than you give me credit for."

Despite my doubts, we applied. We got the job and began jointly leading the Children's and Family ministries at our church. I felt reassured that he was indeed growing spiritually.

That reassurance was short-lived.

"Why are you going to such effort for VBS. No one is

going to show up, anyway. It's just a job; do the minimum and be done with it."

Within a few months he began to complain about going to church on Sunday mornings. I explained that not only did I want our family to go together, it was now part of our job to do so. We were expected to be there. Every Sunday was a fight.

I heard him complain about various kids in our Wednesday night youth group. I asked him to welcome the "difficult" kids and provide them the space a church is meant to be. He'd laugh or groan or say "No. They are just annoying and bad for the morale of the group." I reminded him that we were building a ministry that welcomed neurodiverse people. He'd say, "First, these kids are just annoying, not differently wired. Second, it's just a fucking job we will keep until we have enough money to quit. I don't know why you're looking at this long term. You put in too much effort."

For the most part I stuck to my kids and he stuck to his kids, except during the Christmas Program. It was fun. Until I saw him giving his steely, cold look to a few kids. I saw them hunch their shoulders and lower their eyes. I'd call attention to it after and he'd say, "No. That's the way I have to talk to them or they just won't listen." I'd seen him give that look to parents, as well. Dark, black, soulless eyes sneering at anyone he didn't want to listen to.

Just when I'd feel like I should give up the hope of having any semblance of a family faith life, he'd suggest a prayer time, or feign excitement about church. He gave me hope that God was at work and that I needed to stay faithful.

I'd ask him to help with Sunday school. He'd come, smile in public, sit in the back of the room on his phone, and exude an air of boredom and irritation when we were alone with the kids.

He'd charm the congregants he liked and win them over with his charisma. He seemed loved by many and respected for the work he was doing with the youth, so I held my opinions to myself, covered for him and believed I must be seeing things wrong.

I'd see him joyfully present in the sanctuary and I'd make excuses for the angry fight we'd had right before opening the church doors.

It began affecting my own spiritual life and I realized I needed to let go. To no longer feel responsible for his actions or inactions at church. I explained that I'd be going every Sunday and I would no longer mention it to him. I'd leave it to him whether he brought the kids or not. I couldn't have the arguments anymore.

He'd show up every once in a while, put on the good Christian face and behave in exactly the opposite ways that he would at home. I watched as the youth group deteriorated to his four favorite high school girls. He isolated, shamed and discarded any children he didn't like. He pushed aside any child who didn't feed his ego.

At one point I asked him how he connected with God. I

said that sometimes it's church, but I connect with God when I'm outside in nature or alone at the church playing piano. He said that he connected in youth group and hanging out with the girls. I knew what he did in youth group and it rarely involved anything spiritual. I realized he had no idea what that type of connection felt like. He could not humble himself enough to be connected with God, and instead confused it with the adoration of four young, impressionable girls and the resulting feeling of being God-like. He didn't want to connect with God, he wanted to be God.

Twenty-Two Years

"What's your number?" I asked.

It was the middle of the summer. We'd spent as many nights together as we possibly could. Lying next to each other in post-coital conversation, I braved the question.

"My number?" he said, "Probably not as high as you think it is."

"Okay. So what is it?"

"You tell me first."

"I think I already did. I just had one significant boyfriend before you. You're my second."

"Me too," he said.

"What? No way. I don't believe it."

"Yep. I like to pretend I'm more of a player than I am, but really the emotions mean a lot to me. I wanted to wait for someone special. Turns out I chose the wrong girl. That girlfriend I mentioned before? Yeah, I thought she was special. I went to her place for Christmas and we'd done it a few times, but then she broke up with me. She was done."

"Really? Did you want to be done, too?"

"No. It was awful. But I'm glad it ended so I could meet you."

"You know what?" he added. "She only brought me to finish once. Not like you. With you I don't have any problem finishing. With her I always had to finish myself."

My heart swooned. My insecurities vanished. I couldn't believe how wrongly I'd read him.

Twenty-Six Years

We were back in my hometown, sitting outside sharing drinks and engaging in ordinary talk. Somewhere along the way he said, "I've had just one one-night-stand." He continued but my ears closed off. What? One night stand?

"You told me you'd only been with one person?" I sheepishly asked.

"Oh. Right." He backpedaled. "I guess I don't really count that or I must have forgotten about it or something."

"Okay fine. Here's your chance. Come clean. What's your actual number?"

"Just those two. I swear."

"If I find out there's been more and you weren't upfront with me now . . . ." The empty threat dangled off the incomplete sentence. He remained quiet.

It didn't add up, but I let it slide. I didn't want to know.

Twenty-Seven Years

He spoke a lot about a girl at work. I couldn't quiet my suspicions. I asked him about it, and he laughed and said that he was not even close to being attracted to her. He set us up to go out with her and her husband.

We had fun. Went to dinner and a concert. She was sweet and smitten. With my husband. Her husband was a jackass.

On the drive home I voiced my observations and concerns to him. I asked him to be careful. As a full-time grad school student I didn't have a lot of spare time to give him attention. She did. And she clearly was falling for him. He said I had nothing to worry about and seemed to feel flattered by "my jealousy."

The following day he said, "Funny thing. Her husband said he could really tell how much I loved you. So that should make you feel better."

It continued. We spent a few times together as couples. Then it stopped. I'd suggest getting together and he would avoid it. I knew something was off. I knew he was cheating with her.

I found a picture of her hidden away in one of his books. I asked him about it. He came up with some lame excuse.

He started complimenting me a lot and initiating time together. We started going out for weekly dates. Friday nights spent at the local Italian place, drinking, eating and smoking. We would walk to the cinema to watch a movie while our buzz wore off, then drive home and have sex. He was attentive and supportive.

I couldn't shake the feeling, though. One morning I woke up to my husband running out of the apartment door and down the steps. I heard yelling between two men. I looked out the window and saw her husband yelling at my husband.

He came back upstairs. I asked him what that was about. He said her husband has accused him of fucking his wife. My husband lied. Said it never happened. I held my ground. He came up with some lame excuses. I held my ground. He admitted it. In a completely ass backwards sort of way. He said he wanted it to end and he wanted to tell me, but he didn't know how. He said that it had only been once, a few times, maybe ten. He said they fucked in my car, in my spare bedroom ("but never in our bed! I wouldn't be that disrespectful"). He said he wished he hadn't done it, but, in a way, it was good because he realized just how much he loved me and wanted to stay with me. He said he'd written a letter to her husband from an anonymous source to tell him what was going on. He'd fabricated a story about seeing them on the bus or something. He said he'd sent it to her husband while she was away in the mountains so she couldn't interfere. He said he was the one that made sure it came out into the open because he wanted it to stop.

I drank a few shots of vodka. I slept for thirty minutes. I woke up still drunk and, without saying a word, grabbed the keys and drove to a nearby store. I bought a pregnancy test, drove back, peed on the stick and waited the requisite three minutes. I looked at it, "shit."

He was knocking on the door wondering what was going on. I showed him the stick. His face smiled, he dropped to his knee and kissed my belly. I grabbed a pack of cigarettes, went outside, smoked the whole pack and drank three appletinis. He suggested I shouldn't do those things for the sake of the baby.

I swallowed my alcohol. Held the cigarette in my hand. Glared at him and said, "I just found out that you cheated and that I'm pregnant. On the same fucking day. Leave me alone."

He said he thought it was God making sure we stay together. He said this pregnancy was a gift and a way for us to start over. I said I couldn't leave and that we'd make it work, but if he cheated one more time that I'd be gone. He said he knew.

We went to counseling.

He went to counseling.

He told me he needed to grieve her absence.

He told me he felt better that it was all in the open.

I told him that I felt worse.

Driving home from a time he actually went to church with me, I said, "You know, she's had a lot of bad shit happen to her. She's vulnerable and you took advantage of that. So you fucked her over and fucked me over." He said, "Thanks for that. That helps me feel better." Somehow talking about his affair ended with me feeling guilty.

He told me that he'd seen her at work and that I'd be

happy to know she'd gained some weight. I said, "Why would that make me happy? Who do you think I am?"

He told me that she was pregnant, but that there was no way it could be his.

He told me she'd had the baby and her husband made her get a paternity test. It was theirs, not my husband's.

Twenty-Nine Years

We'd moved back to my home state. Somehow, I discovered that he was still in communication with her. More than a year later and they were emailing. I yelled and pushed him in his chest. I cried that I'd worked so hard to be forgiving, to move past it and move on, and he was throwing it all back in my face.

He said it wasn't like that. He said that she kept emailing him, but he didn't want to respond. So he asked his friend to cover for him. He said that his friend had taken over his account and was writing to her using my husband's name. He said that he had stayed out of it. He said she'd found out. He showed me the enraged email she sent after she found out she'd been communicating with a fake person.

More cigarettes. More drinking. More yelling and crying. I said I couldn't believe that he could do this to me. He said, "Really? I've lost my best friend over this. He won't even talk to me anymore because of it all."

Late Thirties

As a young child and teen I would sit in the pews on Sunday

morning, half listening to the preaching, and think, "I could do that." I'd listen to public speakers at school assemblies and youth gatherings and think, "I'd love to do that someday." I felt confident in my desire to speak, yet I kept it carefully hidden under layers and layers of shyness and uncertainty while hiding behind my mom at any public gathering.

I'm not entirely sure when it changed, when that quiet exterior stepped aside to let my voice speak out loud, but by my late thirties I was becoming known as an engaging presenter. I began traveling to various conferences and speaking engagements throughout the country. With three small children and a therapy practice, this required coordination on both our parts. Yet, every time I mentioned another opportunity, the answer from my spouse was always, "Yep. Of course. We'll figure it out." I would talk to my friends and coworkers about my supportive husband. He encouraged my professional growth. He never said I shouldn't travel so much. He'd brag about my accomplishments. He'd listen to me speak and then gush over how sexy my brain is. As a words of affirmation girl, I felt loved and appreciated. I did everything I could to get more of it.

I worked hard. I hustled. I built a practice, birthed and raised three children (one with autism and higher needs), spoke, wrote, developed content and pushed myself.

My friends and family pushed me to take breaks and slow down. Strangers said they didn't know how I did it. Coworkers validated my feelings of overwhelm and burnout. My spouse supported, yet minimized my struggle. He grew exasperated if ever I mentioned I was tired or burnt out, or asked for him to step up a little.

"Yeah. Yeah. I know. You're busy."

"I don't get it," I said. "I just want some understanding and compassion. EVERYONE else in the world understands, but the one man who's supposed to be my soft place to land just doesn't seem to get it."

"Well I'm working hard, too, you know. It isn't just all you. Every time you travel, I have to take care of the kids and the house and stuff."

He was right. I should complain less and be more grateful for the mutual sacrifices our family was making. And he did it because he supported me and was proud of my work.

Forty-One Years

"I think we should get a housekeeper."

We'd been concerned about our income to output ratio, but he thought we should pay for a housekeeper. He talked about the mental well-being of walking into a clean house. He talked about how we've struggled to stay on top of the cleaning. He talked about resourcing and delegating the tasks that aren't our strengths.

Two months earlier I had emphasized that since I was homeschooling three children, running a full-time business while also seeing twenty clients a week, keeping up on a weekly blog and podcast, writing a book, building my platform, and managing our daughter's multiple therapies and doctors' visits, that I needed him to be the one fully responsible for the upkeep of the house and the yard. He worked three and a half days a week. He agreed.

As frequently happened, he didn't follow through. He was skilled at saying the words to make the problem go away in the moment, with no intention of actually solving the problem. For two months he complained that he had to do the dishes and the laundry, and that the bathrooms were never cleaned. For two months I reminded him of the conversation we'd recently had. For two months he cooked, shopped and did the dishes, but rarely more.

We hired a housekeeper to come twice a month. He came home from work, cooked dinner, then played video games or read.

And while it seemed unfair, he'd remind me that I like to be busy, that I don't do well when I'm bored and that I chose to do all the things I was doing. That was his favorite. "You're choosing to do all these things. It's not my fault you're choosing to be this busy. I'm not the one that chose to take on all these projects, but I'm feeling like the one that has to sacrifice to make it happen." Never mind that the work I was doing benefitted the family and increased our income.

Every once in a while, he'd praise me, tell me how proud he was of me and brag about me on Facebook, and I felt loved and supported. He'd look at me with the twinkly eyes I remembered from when we were dating and all the hard work was worth it.

Forty Years

"The publisher says I need to grow my audience. So I think I'll start a blog. Any other ideas?"

"I've always wanted to do a podcast, I could do a podcast with you" he said, enthusiastically.

It felt like we were a team that worked together to solve problems. We met as camp co-workers, he volunteered at my workplace, we tackled projects together and this was going to be one more of those projects. A podcast.

We brainstormed names, content and format.

I created the website and researched how to publish a podcast. I set up the RSS feed and submitted it to all the podcast players and apps.

He researched the audio needs and set it up.

We started and did pretty well. People found us funny, helpful, supportive and compassionate. We provided real life empathy and information.

He enjoyed being a podcaster. He'd talk it up to everyone he knew.

We'd sit at the microphones and he'd ask, "What are we talking about today?" I'd respond with a topic.

I told him I'd need him to publish the podcast. I wrote down all the directions, step by step. He did it for a month and then suggested we hire our son to do it.

We'd sit at the microphones and he'd ask, "What are we talking about today?" Eventually I started to respond, 'I'm not sure, what do you think we should talk about?" He'd respond, "It's your thing, I'm just here to provide comedic banter."

We'd be out at dinner with friends and he'd start talking about the positive podcast reviews *his* show was getting.

I'd say it was time to record, and he'd roll his eyes, groan, and say he didn't feel like it.

I suggested recording at different times of the day. He'd do it once or twice and then come up with some reason it didn't work.

He'd tell me he loved doing the podcast together, but he was tired.

He'd tell me he was proud of me and the work. He offered to take charge of the technical side of things and for months we'd have poor sound and a broken microphone or sound board. Every week we recorded he promised me that he'd figure it out. It has yet to be figured out. But, when he was around audio geeks, he'd talk up his knowledge and make sure they knew he was the tech guy for "our" podcast.

I'd say we hadn't recorded for a while or suggest a person to interview and he'd say, "Well, it's *your* podcast. Just tell me what you need and I'll do it."

Twenty-Three Years

We'd just won a gym membership at a silent auction. The cost of the membership was less than $20 a month, which was amazing, because our non-profit salaries wouldn't have been able to afford anything more than that.

It was early evening. I was antsy and wanted to burn off some energy. I changed my clothes, grabbed my keys, and shouted down the short hallway of our two-bedroom apartment that I was going to the gym.

"Wait!" he shouted and came rushing down the hallway.

I thought he couldn't bear for me to leave without a goodbye kiss. Instead, he put on a worried look and told me he didn't want me to go.

"I've just got a bad feeling and I don't want you out driving."

"What? I'll be fine. The gym is only ten minutes away and I really need to get out and do something."

"No, please don't go. Something bad is going to happen. I just know it."

I was about to protest again, when tears fell down his face.

Sobbing he said, "I'm so sorry, My best friend died in a car accident before I went to college and I am so afraid I'll lose you in a car accident, too."

My shoulders and anger dropped as I sighed and said, "Okay. I won't go. But you've got to figure this out, because it feels a little like you're trying to control what I do and don't do, and that's not going to happen long term."

"No, I know. I'm not trying to tell you what to do, I'm just really afraid right now and for some reason my friend just keeps popping up."

"Why haven't you mentioned this before?"

"It's too hard to talk about."

I put my keys down, took off my shoes and stayed in for the night.

And went back to watching television. He never spoke about this friend again.

Thirty-Five Years

I switch on my phone. As each text, missed call and voicemail notification pops up my stomach becomes increasingly knotted.

Fuck. He's been trying to reach me.

I'd just finished a fifteen-hour work day. Eight hours at my day job, six clients at my growing business and an hour commute in between. I was eating on the drive between jobs. I was staying up at night nursing my youngest. I was grieving my dad. I did nothing but work and parent and try to be a good wife.

More than ten text messages starting with a casual greeting and ending in a panicked "CALL ME NOW!!!"

Eight or nine missed calls.

Five voicemails.

Number 1: "Hey, I'm trying to reach you to see what time you'll be home. Let me know."

Number 2: Click.

Number 3: "Where are you? Why aren't you answering?"

Number 4: "Seriously? Why aren't you answering? You know I get worried. I'm imagining you in a ditch or something. I can't believe you aren't getting back to me—so inconsiderate! I need to talk to you! (Angry sigh)" I held the phone away from my ear as I listened to this one because his voice grew louder and louder.

Number 5: Angry sigh. Click.

He'd done all this during my last session of the night. He started about five minutes after my last session started. My session was forty-five minutes long and I turned my phone on within ten minutes after it ended.

I was equal parts pissed and anxious. I was working, what the hell was his problem! I knew I had to call him back. I didn't want to. I knew his rage had only increased as each minute ticked by without me getting back to him.

I dialed his number, held the phone away from my ear and took a deep breath, waiting for him to answer.

"WHERE THE HELL HAVE YOU BEEN? WHY HAVEN'T YOU GOTTEN BACK TO ME?"

"I was in session. I was working and had my phone off."

"I thought you ended earlier!"

"Nope."

"WELL YOU NEED TO BE BETTER ABOUT TELLING ME YOUR SCHEDULE, I'VE BEEN GETTING MORE AND MORE WORRIED. YOU KNOW I GET WORRIED WHEN YOU DRIVE!"

"Okay. Did you need something?"

"Well not now (angry, sarcastic anti-laugh)! You took too long getting back to me, so I had to figure it out myself."

"Okay. I'll be home in about thirty minutes."

"Fine. I put the kids to bed because I didn't know when

you'd be home and if you'd want to say goodnight to them. So, you won't get to see them tonight, I guess. Drive safe." Click.

Twenty-Seven Years

"I just feel so badly for her," he said. He was talking about a friend of his from work who had become a mutual friend. At least, at the time, I thought we were mutual friends. This is the same woman he would sleep with a few months later, but at this time my suspicions were unconfirmed.

"She's had so many miscarriages and I just can't imagine what that must be like. She also told me that she's woken up with her husband on top of her before. Can you imagine? He started having sex with her while she was sleeping. What a perv."

I said, "Well, that's rape. She should really try to get out of that marriage. Even when we're there he doesn't treat her very well."

Early Thirties

The timeline becomes blurred. That happens with trauma. It directly affects the portion of our brains that registers and tracks time. That's why ten seconds of a car crash can feel like ten minutes and something that happened five years ago feels like it happened yesterday.

I don't know when it was, but I opened the computer and found it hadn't been shut down properly. Popups littered the page and the search bar had an address beginning with xxx, so I presumed he'd been looking at porn again. As I closed each popup, I could begin to see the screen beneath. I was surprised to see two men on the screen. Gay porn wasn't typically his style, and my curiosity got the better of me. I clicked the little triangle and heard three men speaking a language other than English and laughing. One was off camera and the other two were standing in front of a bed, naked. As the two men parted, I saw there was a naked female laying on the bed.

I was about to turn it off, when I noticed the men pulling the woman closer to the edge of the bed. She was limp and unresponsive. At first, I thought she might be dead, but then she groggily moved her head to one side, eyes still closed. With horror, I saw one of the men penetrate this unconscious woman. The other jerked off while grabbing her breasts and the third, behind the camera, cheered them on. I froze and nearly threw up. I was watching a rape. These men raped this woman and then posted it for the world to watch. Worse than that, people chose to watch.

My breath caught. *My husband* chose to watch.

I turned it off, shut down the computer and walked away.

Should I say something? Should I confront him? Should I be worried that my husband got off on watching rape?

I did nothing. I said nothing. I asked nothing. I didn't really want to know.

Late Thirties

"Can you believe this entitled bastard got such a short sentence for raping a woman behind a dumpster?!"

I was appalled. Six months, only three of which were served, given to a privileged young man who was seen inserting something into an unconscious woman. He stopped only because two passersby did the right thing and intervened. There is no better example of rape culture than for a man to presume he can put any part of himself, or anything else, inside a woman simply because she has passed out.

Early Forties

I don't know when it shifted, but it did. This man I'd lain next to for nearly twenty years became more forceful, more subtly aggressive.

He'd wait for me to roll over to go to sleep and then ask, "Wanna have sex?"

If I said no, he'd get irritated and roll away from me, saying something like, "Of course you don't."

If I said, "I really need more warming up than that." He'd sigh and say, "You can just say no, you know." We'd had this conversation a million times over the years. "I need to feel connected," I'd say. "I need a little foreplay. I need to feel like you actually want *me* and not just to have an orgasm. Say nice things. Spend time with me. Give me kisses on my neck. Anything other than just watching tv until you roll over and say 'Wanna have sex.'"

Most of the time he'd pretend to listen, maybe make a half-hearted attempt to connect, and I'd give in. Sometimes he'd say he'd try and then just go to sleep. Lately, his strategy had changed.

"You keep saying that, but how am I supposed to do it? I can't get to your neck because you're always wearing a sweatshirt to bed. You sit there watching your Kindle or playing on your phone. How am I supposed to show you interest and do any foreplay when that's what you give me?"

Or,

"I have! I've tried giving you more attention and it doesn't change anything, so what's the point?"

For the record, he might have initiated a conversation in the kitchen at one point. Supposedly, that was him trying.

Or,

"It's funny that it's always me that needs to change. What about you? You haven't done anything to try to give me what I need!"

For the record, I intentionally bought him gifts, asked how his day was, listened to his stories, had sex daily with him for a stretch until he stopped it, initiated more often, encouraged the thirty minute I-lead sessions.

Other than just responding differently when I asked for more connection, he changed strategies in other ways too. Sometimes when I said no to his oh-so-sexy "Do you wanna have sex?" he'd start pressuring. He'd say, "Oh, c'mon, it's been a while." or "C'mon, I can convince you." and start touching me between my legs.

I'd slapped his hand away at one point and said, "What's happening? That's one thing that I've always appreciated about you. You've never pressured before. You always respected me when I said no. Why is that changing?!"

He had no response and just rolled away.

When I said yes, he'd be more forceful than usual. Sex didn't feel loving any longer, it felt angry. He had a look on his face that I couldn't describe, but was unsettling. I couldn't look at that face so I would pinch my eyes closed and either check out, imagine a friendlier version of him, or just focus on the physical sensations. He would make forceful grunts that he'd never made before. I felt used or belittled and I couldn't entirely figure out why. In the morning I felt sore and bruised, like my pubic area had been repeatedly punched.

I don't remember the first time it happened. I can't remember the order of events. And while the following may be a fictitious chronology, each memory is exact and filled with the emotions and physical impressions that verify its truth.

I woke up to him groping my breasts and thrusting against me. I was clothed. He was clothed. And yet I felt my body being violated.

I flashed back to an experience at a small, inner city convenience store. I had just begun to grow more comfortable with my body thanks to the compliments and encouragement of my young spouse. I was wearing a tight t-shirt and jeans. A man with a skeevy, toothless smile and gnarled fingers reached out, touched my breast and mumbled a question. I couldn't understand him so I said, "Excuse me?" He touched my nipple and mumbled a question. I said, "Please stop touching me." He brushed my nipple again and mumbled something. I said, "Stop touching my breast!" He walked out of the store laughing.

I moved away and rolled onto my stomach. My husband stopped. We both fell asleep.

The next morning I asked him not to touch me while I slept.

I woke to him with his hand down my underpants. I wasn't sure what to do. My body responded the way a body is designed to respond to sexual stimuli. So, half asleep, I let it happen.

I woke to him with his hand down my underpants. I wasn't sure what to do. I lay still. He continued. My body responded. And then I started to cry and kicked his arm away.

"Geez. Are you ok?" he asked incredulously.

"No. Yes. I don't know. I just feel really scared or something. I'll be ok."

He rolled over. I rolled over, clutched my pillow and quietly cried myself to sleep.

I woke to him with his hand on my breast. Still half asleep I went with it. After I climaxed, he rolled over. I felt gross inside, but didn't know why. I reached for him and said I felt bad that he didn't get any pleasure. He said that he just liked making me achieve orgasm. I was confused. He wasn't listening to my requests not to touch me while I was sleeping, and yet he wasn't getting any sexual pleasure in it. While it didn't feel like it was for me, it must have been for me. What was wrong with me that I wasn't appreciating it?

I woke to him touching my thigh and asking in a whisper if I was asleep. I wondered what would happen if I just stayed asleep. Certainly he'd move back to his side of the bed.

I said nothing. I didn't move. I didn't move when he stroked my thigh. I didn't move when he slid his hand under my waistband. I didn't move when he shoved his fingers inside of me. I pretended to be asleep. He did what he wanted to do. Slowly and quietly he removed his hand from my pants, rolled over and went to sleep as though nothing happened. When I was sure he was sleeping, I rolled over, clutched the mattress and sobbed as quietly as I could.

I woke to him pressing his body against mine and reaching his arm around toward my crotch. I knocked his arm away. He paused for a moment and then reached around again. I knocked his arm away and rolled over to look at him.

"How many times do I need to ask you not to touch me while I'm sleeping?" My anger couldn't be hidden.

"Jesus Christ," he said, "I was just trying to help you feel good."

"But I've asked you not to touch my body and you still do."

"You make me sound like a rapist. God!"

"Well it is a little rape-y, I suppose."

"Oh, I'm just a little rape-y? Don't worry. I won't ever touch you again. I just like giving you pleasure, but if you think that I'm a rapist, Jesus Christ, that's not what I'm doing so, God, I'll just leave you alone."

"No. No. I don't want you to leave me alone. Just wake me up before you start touching me. I don't really know what's going on, but I'm having some strong emotional reactions. I'm wondering if I had some sexual abuse as a kid that I've blocked out of my memory and being touched in the middle of the night is triggering it up or something. It isn't you, it's me, but please just don't for right now."

I lived in his sense of reality to such an extent that it made more sense to create repressed childhood abuse than to understand what actually was happening.

We were in the middle of regular, awake sex. Suddenly I froze with emotion. I pushed him off and asked him to stop. He asked if I was ok. I said, I don't know. He said I should let him know if I need anything and then he walked out of the room.

We were in the middle of regular sex. Suddenly I froze with emotion. I had just recently pushed him off for the same reason and didn't want to do it again because I was sure that would upset him. Instead, I pretended I was into it. He finished. I rolled over, my entire body tense as I hugged my pillow tight and wished I didn't feel so alone.

I noticed I slept on the very edge of our California king. I lay with my back to my husband of nearly twenty years, my arm often hanging off the side of the bed. I went to bed tense and tight every night. I never felt relaxed or safe. I blamed it on being an autism mom. I blamed it on being stressed with my business and mothering. I blamed it on everything but the truth that I didn't feel safe in my own bed. I tried to keep a distance between us as wide as the emotional void I felt.

I woke to him slowly creeping over to my edge of the bed. He gently moved his hand down my side. I moved, still mostly asleep. I felt him pull his hand back He let it dangle in mid-air, waiting for me to settle. As soon as I did, he presumed I was asleep. He moved his hand slowly back. He slowly pulled me over onto my back, making sure not to wake me. He inserted his fingers, thrust a few times, removed them, and rolled back over to his side of the bed.

I woke to him touching me. My body responded. I played along. The next morning I looked at him and said, "You did it again."

"What do you mean?"

"You touched me while I was sleeping again."

"Oh, yeah, but you seemed to like it." he gave me an anti-smile, cold and full of unkind nuance.

"But, I've asked you not to touch me while I'm sleeping."

"Yeah, ok, I forgot. I'll do better."

I couldn't contain it anymore. I burst into tears and shouted, "I just don't understand why it's that complicated. I ask you not to touch me, you don't. Why is it that hard?!"

Blank stare.

"Seriously? What is so difficult about just not touching me while I'm sleeping. It seems like an easy request!"

"I don't always know I'm doing it. It's embarrassing. It's embarrassing every time you bring it up. I think most of the time I'm still asleep and I just do it. I must be having dreams or something. I do know a couple of times you seemed to be having some sexy dreams, so I thought I'd help you out."

"Well you need to talk to someone about that if you're touching me in your sleep. I don't mean to embarrass you, but I need it to stop."

Blank stare.

I left the room and he didn't follow. When I went in later, he was blissfully reading and never mentioned it again. He never apologized.

It's hard to explain. Intelligent, compassionate and a good listener are always among the words people use to describe me. I'm a master's level clinical social worker. I specialize in working with trauma and neurodivergent families. I've advocated for women and against rape culture. I've explained consent over and over again. I've educated men and women on abuse. I know that rape is so much more than a stranger attacking someone at knifepoint. But I couldn't see it.

I knew I felt alone. I knew I tried to be small. I knew that I lived in terror of bedtime, but I couldn't let myself know it all stemmed from sleeping beside a rapist and abuser.

Instead, I clung to the edge of the king-sized bed in an attempt to make myself as small as possible. Curled on my side, knees tucked up to my chest, I gripped the mattress piping. Not knowing how I got there or where "there" even was. Silent tears fell from my eyes, and I prayed that my tears would go unseen, that my husband wouldn't notice. I couldn't move. I couldn't make a noise. I couldn't let myself know who I was living with and how much of me he'd stolen.

PART 2

The Awakening

Like many victims of covert abuse, I always knew something was off and didn't feel right. For a long time, I thought it only felt wrong after we got married. Upon reflection, I see that I knew it, my family knew it, and my friends knew it even before our nuptials.

Over the years I tried to make myself believe that his proposal was sweet and romantic, but I knew it wasn't. If marrying him had been the right thing to do, I wouldn't have felt conflicted. I would have enthusiastically said "Yes!" instead of "Ok." I just said ok.

It was near the end of the summer, a couple of months after we met. Anytime we talked about the future, I'd freak out a little. He and I both constructed the narrative that I was freaking out because I was learning to build trust after it'd been painfully destroyed in my last relationship. That was partially true, but more likely it was the instinctual knowing I'd learned to ignore.

It was one of those nights when the campers were in bed and we had our hour off together. We were out on the soccer field, talking and looking at the stars. Sadness and uncertainty about the upcoming distance between us began creeping in. We were nearing the end of our summer romance and my

Prince Charming would be heading back to England, while I went off to Milwaukee. We didn't know what the future looked like other than the ocean between us.

He had taken to calling any future oriented conversations "scary talk." I thought it was endearing and honored my difficulty with trusting. With hindsight, I see that he engaged in scary talk frequently, disregarding my repeated requests to take things slowly. But that's hindsight, decades, and an enormous amount of learning, later. In the summer of 1999, it was endearing and honoring. He was endearing, honoring, thoughtful and sweet.

On the field that night he said, "Are you ready for some scary talk? I'd ask you to marry me tomorrow if I thought you'd say yes."

It wasn't the first time he'd brought up marriage. I squirmed when he did. On this particular occasion I awkwardly laughed it off and we continued talking.

All the while we were talking my insides were churning and my mind was furiously scrambling. Did I want to marry him? Was this moving too fast? Would I lose him if we didn't commit before departing for our own corners of the world? Is he the man I'd want to be with for the rest of my life? How would I know? What does that feel like? Would he be a good dad? Yes, I think I want to. No, it's too soon. Yes, he's handsome and romantic. No, we're too young. Yes. No. Yes. No.

"I probably wouldn't say no." I blurted out.

"Huh?"

"If you asked me to marry you tomorrow, I probably

wouldn't say no." It was my compromise with my reeling brain. Let him know I'm open to it, but don't fully commit. Spew all the uncertainty out into one sentence and let him decide what to do with it.

I had no idea he'd decide to do what he did.

He dropped immediately to his knee and said, "Heather? Will you marry me?"

I was shocked and still a tornado of emotions and uncertainty. I thought he'd have to take time to get a ring and plan a sweet proposal. I didn't think I would need to back up my own word immediately.

"Ok," I said with a timid little smile.

When I told this story, I would always leave out the conflicted inner turmoil. That wasn't part of a romantic proposal. Instead, I stuck with the words and convinced myself and others that him spontaneously popping the question was exactly what I wanted. Ring be damned.

Part of me knew that marriage wasn't right when I couldn't immediately reciprocate his "I love you." When, after months apart, I picked him up from the international arrivals terminal and felt flat about seeing him, I knew there was just something off.

My best friend took me out to lunch and told me she didn't like him.

My mom asked me if I really knew he was the one.

He lived with my parents the summer before we got married, and my dad brought up his concerns. He asked if I was really sure.

At the end of the aisle, after all the other parents and grandparents, and bridesmaids and men had walked away from us, my dad said, "It's just you and me, Byrd. If this isn't what you want, we can walk away right now. My car's right over there."

And after the wedding, I knew it every time I felt less than or he gave me "the look"—the little sniff and lip turn thing that signaled loathing and disgust. I knew it every time I felt alone.

Yet, I didn't *really* know it. For every soul crushing thing, there seemed to be a positive. He'd cook dinner and I'd think of all the women who complained that their husbands didn't do anything around the house. He'd brag about me and I'd feel flattered. He'd make an effort and do things a little better for a little while.

I invented a reason for every awful thing and responded with empathy and understanding. Of course he yelled; he was stressed about work. Of course he lost his patience with the kids, he's human. Of course he's frustrated when I'm sick or traveling because he *does* have to pull extra duty at home.

I remember talking to my best friend about the ways we'd been hurt or disappointed by our spouses. I don't remember which one of us said, "And we've got good ones! It's so hard for us, imagine what it's like for other women."

He didn't hit or threaten me. He didn't call me names. He didn't overtly control me or try to separate me from friends or family. He wasn't out drinking every night. I wasn't a hunting, golf, or sports widow. He was a good one.

Except he wasn't.

And I knew that. Except I didn't.

Sometime Between 2014 and 2018

Like many abused women, I could tolerate a lot so long as it didn't affect my children. I could make the excuses and find forgiveness. Once I could see the impact of his actions on my kids, though, something sparked. When I saw my children plagued with the same self-doubts and their desperate attempts to please him, I began to see the complete picture.

I don't think this is because I value them more than I value myself. I didn't believe I deserved his treatment and they didn't. No, I could just see it more clearly in them. We can always see things more clearly when we're looking in from the outside. That's part of why therapy works.

Also, I didn't *feel* like I assumed an abused woman would feel. I felt successful. I knew I had a voice and important things to say. I felt independent and strong. I knew I was good at my job and was building success as a speaker and writer. I felt intelligent and optimistic and generally good about myself.

I didn't believe his mood was my fault, and I didn't accept responsibility for the things for which he tried to blame me. Not consciously, anyway.

Yes, there were things about him I didn't like. And there were times when he was mean and intimidating. But he couldn't be abusive because I didn't feel abused.

I just felt lonely, like I didn't matter to him.

I felt unattractive to him and his look cut me to the core.

I felt like I had to do it all in order to keep the house running. I had to be the emotional regulator for the entire household because my kids were kids and my husband wasn't skilled enough to do that. I had to work hard to get what I wanted, but he was a guy, so I couldn't expect things to work differently.

I felt soul weary, but I was busy and a special needs mom. I was sick and exhausted all the time, but I was overweight and overworked. I was anxious, hopeless and stuck, but I'd struggled with depression and anxiety before.

I felt all *those* things, but I didn't feel abused.

I didn't see the abuse because it was a long, slow process and, like many narcissists, he grew worse as he aged. The longer he had me, the more he could get away with and the worse he'd be. The older he was, the more his mask would slip.

I couldn't see the abuse until I saw it impacting my kids.

Shortly after my youngest was born, I read a Facebook meme that said pregnant women crave more chocolate when stressed and that there's a correlation between how much chocolate a pregnant woman eats and how happy the baby is during infancy. I commented that we now knew why my baby was so flipping happy.

Chocolate or not, my youngest smiled and rolled over when he was 3 weeks old and never stopped smiling or moving. Strangers would comment on how happy he was. Family members would say they'd never seen him without a smile on his face. He was a happy, risk-taking, full of life little boy.

I described him as my full-force kid. He never did anything halfway. He'd be jumping and moving, talking, singing, smiling and dancing every waking moment of the day. He told jokes early. He was social and outgoing. He'd go up to random girls on the playground and say, "Hi! Wanna be my girlfriend?" That three-year-old had game. He joyfully attracted people to him.

I watched as this sunny toddler changed. He was an extraordinarily talkative boy. He needed guidance on how to manage this trait of his, but his father's way of guiding him was to hush him, snap his fingers at him and give him the look. "I am talking," he'd say in a disdainful tone of voice. "Be quiet."

One day, after being shushed by his father at the dinner table for the fifty-seventh time, he scrambled down from his chair and I heard his little bare feet patter away. I followed my three-year-old from the table and found him curled up in a corner, eyes covered by his pudgy little preschool hands, crying. He said, "I never should've been born. I don't belong in this family. I just make everything worse."

I saw it more clearly.

A couple years later, when he knew that I was working at home and dad was in charge, he came up to me, apologized for interrupting, said he needed to ask dad for a snack, but he was afraid. His dad was sleeping and my child trembled at the thought of waking him up. For a snack. As a preschooler.

I saw it more clearly.

Then there was my daughter. She has autism, and her version of autism comes with some wicked meltdowns. It's hard on the entire family. Like many an autism mom, I bear the brunt of the dysregulation and all the hard autism things. Partially this is because I'm mom. But it's also because her dad can't handle it and she absolutely does not feel safe melting down in front of him. She's voiced this to me. At first it was, "You're just better at handling it mom." Then it was "I can't melt down in front of him. He gets mad."

I'm human, and I've only got so much bandwidth. There were times I couldn't. I couldn't keep myself regulated. I couldn't physically show up or be the calm, loving presence my daughter needed. In those moments her dad would say he'd take care of it.

He didn't.

I'd hear yells and loud sounds and have no idea what was going on. My daughter would scream during meltdowns no matter what, but when you can't actually see what's happening behind the closed door it's hard to tell what those screams mean.

On many occasions she'd call out for me. And I couldn't. I just couldn't ignore my baby crying for me. So, I'd show up. Rags and all, I'd show up.

He'd glare at me, tell me he had it and intimate that I was being a bad mom for giving in to her. Then he'd storm out.

She'd be crying and screaming, but less in the meltdown way and more in the hurt way. And she'd tell me something hurtful he'd said, or that he threw her doll at her, or that he'd threatened her. I'd help her regulate and eventually mediate a conversation between the two of them.

He would always deny what she said or make up some excuse. When I'd confront him and say, "She said you slapped her," he'd say, "Do you really think I'd do that?" His incredulous anger and gaslighting would confuse me. I believed my daughter, but I wasn't there and I'd never seen him hurt her. How could I know for sure?

I would try to ride the line. I would not dismiss my daughter, but also not accuse my husband of lying.

One time I helped regulate her and then asked if she wanted me to bring dad back in. She said, "There's no point. He's just gonna lie and say he didn't do it anyway."

I saw it more clearly.

My friends, my family and his family all made unfavorable comments about how he reacted to our daughter. They softened their criticism with comments like, "Well, yeah, but you can't be mad at her, can you? It's not her fault." or "Huh. Not much good to say about her today?" But they saw it.

I saw it more clearly.

Two of the times that really drove it home for me involved my oldest son. He's always been bright, empathic, intuitive. He knew things before he had words to express them.

One day he mentioned how his dad dealt with people who annoyed him.

"You know, how he is sarcastic and makes fun of them,

but in a way that the person doesn't realize he's making fun of them?"

That one made me see more clearly. It made me see what my kids saw. He was their dad, their model of who a good man, a good dad should be. Was this what I wanted for my children?

He did often play with our kids. He joked and made them laugh. He played video games with them and read to them. He cooked them their favorite foods and made them special treats. He was a hands-on dad. I can't say whether this made him a good dad or not. Ultimately, that's up to his children to decide. But I can say that it confused me. It kept me from acknowledging all the abusive things he'd do to me. And it kept me from seeing the potential harm that could bring to my kids.

The following incident is what really opened my eyes.

It was July 2019. My oldest and I were in Houston for a conference and speaking engagement. I loved these trips. One on one time with my maturing son. He'd help me out at the exhibition hall booth and we'd be sure to do some fun things together wherever we'd traveled.

We were leaving Houston and on the way to the airport. Our timeline was tight when I realized I'd forgotten my debit card in the hotel room.

My initial reaction? Shit.

My second reaction? How the hell can I resolve this right now? I couldn't turn around because we needed to make our flight and I didn't have the card or a way to look up the phone number to call and cancel the card.

I decided that I had to call my husband and ask him to call the hotel and the card company.

This was absolutely not an easy decision.

I'd been yelled at for mistakes like this before. I'd heard the groans of frustration and outright refusal to do things that inconvenienced him before. And while there was never any direct name calling, the unspoken words were there.

The only saving grace was that I at least wouldn't have to see his eyes.

I told my son I was gonna call dad. He took a deep breath, tucked his feet up on his seat, clutched his knees to his chest and braced himself.

I noticed this, but didn't want to put my experience and anxiety onto him, so I left it and hit dial.

The call went surprisingly well. There was a sigh and a slight irritated voice, but no blaming. No shaming. He said he'd take care of it.

I was surprised and exhaled a breath I didn't know I was holding.

I looked over at my son, still sitting in a tight ball. He also let out a breath and said, "Well that didn't go as bad as I thought it would."

I saw it all too clearly.

I saw the home I was living in and the relationship I was staying in. I clearly saw the man with whom I was coparenting. We were living in a constant pressure cooker, in constant anxiety. Calling about a forgotten credit card should not create such intense anxiety. My son should not feel it and expect the yelling. My kids saw more than I had realized. They felt more than I had known. If it was soul-wearying for me, what was it doing to the three precious parts of my heart that lived outside of me?

I could label the harm. I didn't yet call it abuse, but I could label it as definitely not ok. It was damaging me and my children. It was unacceptable and needed to change. I was waking up.

2018

"I'm pretty sure my mom and my ex are covert narcissists."

My client looked at me from across the therapy room. I nodded and said something like, "What have you seen to make you think so?" On the outside I was acting with confidence. Yep! Of course I know what covert narcissism is! On the inside I was thinking. Thinking that I understood the word covert. It meant flying under the radar. And I know what narcissism is. According to the DSM-5 (the manual used by all mental health professionals to diagnose psychiatric concerns), narcissistic personality disorder is a "pervasive pattern of grandiosity (in fantasy or behavior), a constant need for admiration, and a lack of empathy." Internally, I was trying to figure out how those two things go together, but figured I'd look it up later and turn my attention back to my client.

Like many things that I intend to look up later, I completely forgot about it.

At this point, I'd begun noticing the issues with the way my kids responded to my husband. I'd begun talking to him in private about what I was seeing. I'd reflected that he seemed to be agitated a lot and maybe therapy would be helpful. I'd written letters to him hoping that would clarify things and motivate him to make parenting changes or heal himself. I'd suggested date nights and asked for what I needed. I had pleaded with him to at least not talk badly about the church in front of the kids, and to not grumble when one of the kids wanted to play a board game. I'd tried to be less self-focused and be consciously kind and attentive to him. I'd done the nightly sex thing. I'd talked about love languages. I'd talked and asked and pleaded. Every time, I ended in the same place of disappointment, rejection and tears.

I remember telling my friend that I just didn't know what to do anymore. I remember telling her that it seemed like nothing worked. If I asked for what I needed, he'd promise to do it and then never follow through. If I gave him more attention, I created a monster who wanted even more and grew even more self-centered. If I ignored him, he would pout. If I initiated sex, he'd stop wanting it. If I mentioned that he seems kind of crabby, he would say it's because he hadn't had sex for a while.

Nothing worked.

I heard myself talking and realized how much of my

focus was centered on him and his happiness. I saw how much of my own wellness and emotional state centered on him and his emotional state.

I remembered our hiking trips and how he would always ruin them. For our anniversary one year, we'd gone to stay in the mountains and, on one of the days, I wanted to take a hike. We'd recently bought a new-to-us car. I'd found a trail in a guidebook that ended at a waterfall and headed in the direction of the trailhead. Never having been to this trailhead before, I didn't know it was down a progressively narrowing road that became more rugged and less paved the further we went.

The grumbling began. Whenever something went worse than planned it was commonplace for him to complain, pout, yell, declare it wasn't going to work and demand that we stop. This was especially true when the activity was for someone other than himself. If it was something he wanted, he'd find a workaround. If it was something I wanted, he was ready to throw in the towel before it even began.

And so, as we drove down the road in the newest and most luxurious car we'd owned to that point, the road narrowed and grew bumpier.

"This is a bad idea. I knew this was a bad idea. We should turn around and go back. What a stupid idea."

"I'm not sure we can turn around. It isn't wide enough for that. We'll just have to keep going because I'm not reversing the whole way out," I reasoned.

"Didn't you look this up before we came?! I can't believe

we're driving our new car on this shithole of a road. It isn't even a road. Why did you pick this one?!"

I inhaled to keep myself calm, then I saw a car coming from the opposite direction.

"Shit! Now what are you going to do?! I knew this was a bad idea. Going into the middle of the fucking wilderness and now we're going to be stuck."

I pulled over as far as I could. The other car pulled over as far as they could. There was just enough room to squeeze by. Unfortunately, the ground yielded just enough room, but there were some tree branches that hung low into the roadway.

I heard them scratch against the car. I held my breath.

The rage released.

"Fucking hell! Pull over! You should've turned around or made them back up. What the fuck?! We JUST got this car and now it's going to look like shit. Pull over!"

I reasoned that I'd rather get to the trailhead since there wasn't a lot of space on the road and if there were any scratches, they'd still be there to look at once I found a parking space.

Fumes and simmering rage oozed from the passenger seat.

The road widened and ended at a small grass parking lot. We got out. There were a few minute scratches on the side of the door. I could barely see them.

"I can't believe it. For a fucking hike. We can't ever have nice things and keep them nice. We've had this car for two fucking days and now it looks like shit."

"We can always patch it or get them buffed out."

"Are you kidding me? That's always a bigger and more expensive job than it seems. Nope. It's just ruined. All of our nice things get ruined."

"Well, the car still works well, nobody is hurt, and they're pretty small scratches. I bet no one will even notice them."

"I can't believe you don't care about this!" he screamed. "It'd be nice if you gave a shit about our stuff. And I don't care what other people think. I know it's there and I just want to have something nice for once."

I headed off to the trail and started hiking. He kept complaining.

He amplified his usual grumbling about rocks, the weather and bugs with sorrow and rage over the car, our material possessions and how unfortunate we were.

I'd recently learned about differentiation in a graduate course I was taking for my MSW. Differentiation allows a person to care for someone else, but not take responsibility for that other person's thoughts, behaviors, or feelings. To be close, but still know that you're an independent individual and can have your own thoughts and feelings.

As I felt my mood spiral from the incessant grumbling, I decided to try something different. Just because he was miserable didn't mean I needed to be. I was going to try to differentiate.

"I understand you're upset and in a bad mood, and that's fine. I get it. But, it's a beautiful day. We're in a beautiful spot in the mountains and it's a gorgeous hike that I want to enjoy. So, I'm just going to hike a little faster and a little further up than you. If you can enjoy the hike too, I'd love for you to catch up. Otherwise, I'll be content hiking on my own."

Off I went.

It took me a few hundred yards, but I calmed. My breathing slowed. I heard the birds and the river, and smelled the fresh mountain air. I felt the sun warm my body and melt the racing, anxious thoughts right out of my brain. I enjoyed my hike.

It had worked. Intentional differentiating had worked. He eventually calmed down and by the time we got to the waterfall we were able to have a pleasant talk and hike peacefully back to the car.

If differentiation had worked all those years ago, perhaps I needed to apply it more to my life in the present.

I decided I was going to intentionally focus less on catering to him, and more on rediscovering myself.

I had stopped doing a lot of the things that had previously fed my soul. I wasn't playing the piano or even listening to music. I wasn't writing. I was adopting his judgmental eye and snarky sarcastic humor. I was looking for shortcuts at work and developing a bad attitude toward the church. Truthfully, I was developing a bad attitude toward almost everything. I didn't like this version of myself.

My first step was to tell him that I was done fighting about church. I told him I was going to go every Sunday. I would ask the kids to come with me, but I would no longer pester him to go too. He could have whatever attitude he wanted about church and show up whenever and however he wanted. I was going to do my job and enjoy it. He was welcome to come whenever he wanted, but I was no longer going to ask him.

I had come to radically accept that his attendance wasn't up to me. I'd told him it was important to me, and I'd asked, begged and yelled to try to make church-going a family thing. He would blatantly fight against it. He would tell my oldest that he wouldn't like youth group so he shouldn't even try it. He would complain about church and the people that attended in front of the kids. I later learned from my daughter that every Saturday night he would suggest that she say she didn't want to go or that it'd be too much for her to go and then he'd stay home with her. In reality, my daughter did want to go, but she would do as her dad wanted.

None of it was up to me. I could be responsible for bringing the kids, or do my own thing, but I couldn't stop him from sabotaging it.

The moment I gave up that idea, the moment I stopped making excuses for why he wasn't at church, was the moment I began to find church meaningful again. It was the moment I began to forge deeper relationships with the people at the church and to reconnect with my faith. I let him do him and focused more on what was right for me.

As I did that, other things fell into place. I began going to the church at night to play the piano and pray. I began writing more. I started dancing and singing in the living room. I started coloring and reading and baking again. I was feeling more alive than I had in years.

This was also the time he became crueler and when the sexual assaults began. He could sense I was feeling freer, so he stripped me down even further.

2019

Hiding in my closet I was talking to my best friend on the phone. I had to confess. I had to tell her that I was building an increasingly strong attraction to someone and I was fairly certain it was mutual. I told her I didn't want it, but I also loved feeling interesting to a man again. I loved feeling seen. I didn't understand where this was coming from. I was completely in love with my husband and he was such a good man. I didn't understand why I'd be pulled toward something outside of my marriage.

My best friend responded with the question that saved my life.

She asked, "Well, what does he have that you are missing in your relationship with your husband? What are you attracted to that maybe your spouse doesn't have?"

I didn't immediately have an answer. But the question simmered and stuck with me and, eventually, I found my answer. I found about five hundred different answers, actually. This question woke me up.

What was different?

This man and I conversed. He made eye contact and listened and seemed genuinely interested in what I had to say.

My husband talked. Usually he talked at me. Sometimes he talked while in the middle of doing other things. He rarely listened to me. He would literally walk out of the room while I was talking about something important to me. But he'd yell over his shoulder, "Keep going, I can hear you!" and I would tell myself that he was interested, just busy. I would tell myself it was just that we'd been together for 20 years and that infatuated phase of the relationship was over. I'd tell myself we were busy with kids and tired from autism parenting, and remember the times over the years when he did listen. I'd tell myself this was normal. Until I interacted with this man who actually conversed.

This man thought. He thought about intellectual, academic topics or his own behaviors or the dynamics around him. He reflected.

My husband shut down any conversation that started to get too reflective. "I don't have the energy for this," he'd say. He'd refuse to consider that he might have reason to reflect on himself, and his own behaviors and ways they needed to change. If ever I mentioned something hurtful or how his parenting was having a negative effect on the kids, he would play victim. "Yep. It's always me. I'm always the bad one who does everything wrong," he'd say and walk away. I'd start questioning myself. Was I being too hard on him? What role did I play? How could I improve?

This man put in effort. He went above and beyond to be helpful to anyone, with no strings attached. He did his best, worked hard and strove for excellence. When excellence was achieved and someone commented, he would humbly thank them and move on to a new topic.

My husband always put in the least amount of effort possible. He'd find loopholes and shortcuts and ways to cheat the system. In one of his earliest jobs he joined the safety committee, "because it looks good and I don't really have to do anything for it." He wanted the most recognition and gain for the least effort.

This man helped me grow. He challenged me to be a better person and gently helped me see that some of my thinking and behaviors were unhelpful. There was no judgment or shaming in the process.

My husband chided, mocked and shamed, but he never actually helped me to grow. I knew I wasn't perfect and I wanted to have a partner who gently confronted me. What I received was either shame and loathing, or apathy and distance.

This man walked beside me and adjusted his pace to match mine.

My husband consistently walked three to six feet in front of me. He joked that my short legs couldn't keep up.

But most astonishingly, this man never exploded. He was calm and steady. I'd seen him angry. I'd seen him frustrated with injustice and the behaviors of others. He could be firm and voice his opinion. He could be angry. But his eyes remained kind. His voice remained unintimidating. His body language remained peaceful and unthreatening. There was no look. No rage. No out of control yelling and slamming of things.

I truly, honestly, didn't know this kind of man existed.

My dad was explosive though he didn't always yell. Often his explosiveness came in the form of cold, punctuated sentences accompanied by the look. My husband was loudly explosive. Something went wrong and he'd fly off the handle. The look, the rage, the yelling, the quiet menacing voice. All of it.

It wasn't until my friend asked her question that I began to consider what I was seeing and experiencing with this man, and how much what I saw contradicted all the things I'd grown accustomed to believing about men. My lived experience told me men were naturally going to be explosive. Either quietly or loudly, but intimidatingly nonetheless. Men would flip out when things didn't go the way they wanted and it was up to women and children to accommodate the explosiveness or try to prevent it.

Of course, on reflection, I knew this wasn't true. I'd known calm men. I'd known kind-eyed and soft-hearted men. But my brain could dismiss them as anomalies in favor of maintaining the hard-wired belief that I shouldn't and couldn't feel seen and safe around a man.

The answer to my friend's question was that I was attracted to kindness, and I didn't have that in my marriage. I hadn't believed it even existed.

My husband and I were going on a short trip to California. I hadn't yet seen our relationship for what it was, but I had recognized the lack of empathy, care or kindness I got from him.

Over the past months I'd told him I felt disconnected.

I'd told him I needed more quality time and positive words. I'd told him that I was starting to have sex dreams about other men. I had hope that we could make changes and create the environment of conversation, reflection, growth, steadiness and kindness that attracted me. Part of me now saw the man I'd married much more clearly; another part was still the eternal optimist and ready to keep fighting.

    We headed into the airport. Within minutes I was silently crying. We were standing in line to check our baggage. True to form, my husband moved into the line before me, without even acknowledging I was there. He stood looking forward. I stared at his back. Neither his shoulders nor his hips were turned toward me. He didn't stand sideways. He had slung his bag over his shoulder, squared his body and closed me out. I was upset, but then began to wonder if maybe I was making too big of a deal of this. Maybe this isn't abnormal. Maybe I'm, once again, being "too sensitive." I glanced at the other passengers waiting in line. I could easily identify who was traveling with whom. Body language created small elongated circles of people, chatting, smiling, maybe checking their phones, but still facing each other. Had anyone looked in my direction, they would have seen 2 independent travelers. A 6'4" man looking straight ahead, and a sad looking female a few feet behind him, staring longingly at his back.

    I sent a photo to my friend. She immediately empathized. She knew that I had asked him to be more attentive. That I'd asked for him to take this trip to reconnect and give me that quality time I so desperately need in order to feel loved. She knew how lonely I felt staring at his back and how unimportant I felt. She knew how painful it was that I had asked explicitly for what I needed, and he still didn't give it to me.

The entire trek through security and to the gate remained silent and alone. We got settled at the gate and he started to talk. My ever-hopeful heart perked up. He said, "You know, if you weren't here, I'd be able to talk my way into first class."

I smiled and pretended to check my email.

The trip to California was part "pleasure" and part business. We were exhibiting at a conference and instead of bringing my oldest child, decided we'd try this trip to reconnect. As soon as the conference started, my husband turned to me and said, "Well, it doesn't make sense for both of us to sit here at the table together doing nothing. How about we take it in shifts?" And that was it. Our trip to reconnect turned into a solo trip where we happened to share the same room at night and an occasional meal in the evening.

When it came time to board the flight home, not only did I receive his back again, but he literally pushed his way to the front of the line, not even recognizing that I had been separated from him. He boarded the plane about 15 people ahead of me.

"Seriously?" I said. "You just left me."

"I had to get on to make sure there was going to be space for our things in the overhead compartment."

"You didn't even consider me. And there'll always be

space on the plane for our things. There isn't anything we need immediate access to."

"Yes, but I didn't want to have to wait in order for the plane to empty so I could grab my bag that would have been ten rows behind me if I'd waited for you. I'd do the same thing again."

After we got home I tried to make excuses for this behavior. I labeled it anxiety. He said he wasn't anxious. I didn't believe him. I had to have some sort of explanation other than just plain rudeness and disregard for my presence. I said it must be anxiety because you were worried about not having enough space on the plane. He said he wasn't worried about it, he just wanted what he wanted and was going to make sure he got it.

At that moment I couldn't believe it. But, in the next few months, I started looking into covert narcissism. I'd started to read about it for the sake of my client, but also because some of the stories and behaviors she was describing sounded familiar to me. As I was reading, I looked back on this situation and realized he was telling the truth. He wasn't anxious at all. He was simply a narcissist who was no longer trying to hide who he was around me. He didn't have to hide anything. He was getting away with emotionally, psychologically, financially and sexually abusing me and I was still telling the kids they never had to worry about their parents divorcing because I didn't believe in divorce. I was all in. He'd spent his time priming me for just these moments. These moments when his true disturbed character could ooze out and I would simply make excuses and move on.

With the realization that not every man behaves the way my husband did, I began questioning more things. I began questioning the reality I'd been groomed to accept.

Aside from the fight every Sunday about church, there'd also be a fight every Sunday about Sundays themselves. He'd complain every Sunday. He'd complain that our daughter ruined them. He'd complain that Sundays were supposed to be relaxing, but instead he's having to deal with meltdowns and bullshit.

Sundays *were* hard. During the years when we were learning to understand my daughter, the afternoons would regularly be filled with meltdowns. Awful, gut wrenching, aggressive, tear-spilling meltdowns. In response, he would yell, scream and threaten, so I made sure to be the one who helped my daughter through those rough days.

On several occasions, he commented that I spent too much time with her. He said that he felt bad for our youngest because I neglected him while caring for our daughter.

One of the things moms of autistic children feel the guiltiest about is the impact on their other children. We can't be the kind of mom we want to be because we're trying to keep everyone safe, running to appointments, or simply exhausted from the constant hypervigilance and stress. We worry that our other children feel neglected.

Many clients correlate therapist with good mothering.

They hold the false belief that by virtue of my vocation, I must have all this parenting stuff figured out. I regularly remind them that there is only one difference between me and them: I have the theories to *really* beat myself up about fucking up my children. Of course I had the same feelings of guilt and worry they did. I still do. I worry I'm not capable of giving enough to my sons. I grieve that every birthday is tainted by autism.

My husband knew that.

He knew exactly how sharp the knife was when he subtly called me a bad mom to my boys.

The painful irony is he also knew I had to be the primary caregiver for my daughter. He couldn't do it. I knew our son felt more connected to me than to his dad. His comment was angering, shaming and highlighted a double-bind he had partially created.

His negativity could be infectious. I began to dread Sundays. He would blame our daughter. I would blame autism. As I woke up, I began to doubt that autism was wreaking havoc on our Sundays and see that it was something else.

Contrary to popular belief, most autistic people do not lack empathy. Most autistic people I know have too much empathy. They feel the energy of the room and the emotions of others to the extent that they cannot tell which are their own feelings and which belong to someone else. They become overwhelmed and emotionally dysregulated as they soak in all the emotions of all the people around them.

Coming to this knowledge had me reflecting on Sundays.

Most often, my daughter would wake up in a good mood. If she went to church, I'd spend some time helping her regulate her sensory system after. And then, somewhere along the line, she'd go off the rails.

My husband, on the other hand, would most often wake up grumbling, negative and irritable on a Sunday morning. He'd either go to church and grumble or sit disengaged in the corner of the room, or he'd stay home and let out a sigh when we returned. He'd grumble about "waiting for it to kick off" and he'd be short and curt with the kids and me. If we tried to do something fun, he'd say it was going to go awfully because of our daughter and he'd either talk me out of it or go along with a pissy attitude. If we tried having a quiet day at home, he'd yell if a child attempted to wake him or refuse to play a game or grumble about playing a game.

Of course there were some fun times on some Sundays. There were video game tournaments and movie nights and reading together out on the porch. But those Sundays were far outnumbered by the negative, black rain cloud, meltdown Sundays. I regularly had to regulate both my daughter and my husband.

I tried talking to him about my growing insight. I tried getting him to see that when he started the day with a bad attitude, it would influence the rest of the day. I'd emphasize how big his influence was on the climate of our home. He'd deny it. Or blame our daughter. He'd tell me I was wrong. He'd make a snide comment and I'd say, "That. That's what I'm talking about. You seem angry." He'd angrily say he wasn't angry and give me a glimmer of the look, a foreshadowing of what would be unleashed if I pushed it any further.

With these denials and his projecting onto and scapegoating our daughter, I'd lost confidence in my ability to understand him and his emotions. I'm a fucking therapist. A pretty good one with a strong intuition and the empathy to identify what clients are and are not saying and feeling. I knew he was angry. But he said he wasn't. So, I doubted myself.

During the summer of 2019 I led a weekend camp for families with children on the autism spectrum. The camp brochure listed us both as leaders, but it was me. I did the work. I led all the activities. I prepped everything.

In the days leading up to the camp he'd asked, with his game controller in hand, if I needed help. I'd long ago learned not to ask for help, so I said I didn't think so. He said I should let him know if I think of anything. A couple of hours later, the craft prep was taking longer than I anticipated. I asked him to help me. He immediately gave me the look of loathing, said he was getting ready for bed, sighed and added, "I already asked you and you said no. If you needed my help, you should have asked then."

As I had been trained to do, I told him to never mind.

He persisted, most likely so he could talk about being the grand helper in the future, and started to cut things out. He complained, and sighed, and brought with him a dark, negative, disdainful energy. He picked fights. He made it so miserable that after ten minutes I told him to go to bed. I told him he was making it worse and I'd rather stay up later and do it on my own. He quickly set the scissors down, said in a faux perplexed voice "I said I could help, but whatever, if you don't want me to . . ." and walked away.

That was the extent to which he "helped" lead the weekend. Whenever he talked about the camp, though, he took credit. He'd say, "I led this autism camp last weekend." It infuriated me, and yet it felt too petty to correct him. Partially it infuriated me because he not only didn't help, but he made the weekend more difficult.

I'd agreed that I'd lead most of the activities and asked that he be primarily responsible for our daughter. I couldn't be responsible for the entire flow of the weekend and for meltdown management simultaneously.

While my daughter was regulated, all went smoothly. Being out of routine, filled with excitement, new people, new activities, and all sorts of challenge, it was expected that she'd have a meltdown or two.

During one such instance, we were at a bonfire by the lake. We were making smores, chatting with people and enjoying the summer night. It was the first time I was able to relax and not be in charge of something all weekend. My daughter started to go into the lake and refused to come out. He started yelling at her. It was unsuccessful. She started using the voice that indicates she's in meltdown mode and there's a slight chance of return. I came over to help. She flipped. Not literally in the water, but her brain flipped into total meltdown and she was no longer in control of her body. He stormed off and said, "God! I almost had it and then you had to come over! You deal with her then!"

In one fell swoop he dehumanized my daughter, abandoned both of us when we needed him and blamed me for her meltdown.

I managed to get her up to my room. My friend was also at the camp and took care of my boys while I attempted to regulate my daughter and her dad said things like, "Just stop! You're embarrassing yourself! You're embarrassing your mother and I. Do you see how you're hurting your mom? We were having a good day, don't ruin it." etc., etc., etc.

Later my friend said she was sitting outside our room in case anything was needed and she started to cry when she heard him. She said incredulously, "Doesn't he understand she has autism and isn't doing it on purpose?"

I am so thankful for that camp. It fully opened my eyes. It was painful and harsh, but necessary and provided cornerstone memories that I could go back to whenever I doubted who he actually was.

We were at the archery range. Our six-year-old was having difficulty getting the arrows near the targets. I can't remember what his dad said, but I know he mocked him. My son had been a risk taker, but quickly learned that the smaller he was the safer he was. He tried to shrink in space and his confidence shrunk with him. He was a born perfectionist. This is the kid whose dad mocked him when he couldn't get an arrow close to the target. His father then attempted to give him some half-assed advice, pretending he knew more about archery than he did.

When it was my husband's turn, he missed the target. Reflexively I laughed and made a joke about how I thought he was the archery expert. I'm not proud of the cruel humor I inherited from twenty years with my husband, and I've intentionally been changing it. We can have jokes and be light-hearted with each other without the need for making jokes at someone else's expense. That particular time, however, I probably did mean for the joke to cut a little. I felt protective of my littlest guy and I wanted his dad to shut up.

My husband and I approached the target to gather the arrows. As I was pulling mine out, he pretended to grab one, leaned close into my face, sniffed, glared, and whispered through gritted teeth so chillingly and threateningly my heart still stops as I think about it, "Don't you *ever* make a fool of me again." He walked away, leaving me frozen in fear.

Like anyone accustomed to living with terror, loathing and shame, I shook it off, plastered on a smile, and turned back to my son enthusiastically shouting, "Your turn again bud! You've got this!" without so much as hinting anything had happened.

The other life changing event happened on our last morning. My daughter was tired, overdone and needed extra rest. Her dad stayed with her and I went to breakfast with the boys and the rest of the camp. About halfway through breakfast, I heard the dining hall door slam and he brusquely crossed the room, leaned down near me and slapped a credit card on the table. The look, the tone, the energy, told me immediately I'd done something wrong.

"Don't you check your texts?!"

I told him I never got a text. It's camp and the reception was awful.

"I've tried calling and texting you and you're just ignoring me. Your daughter could have needed something!"

"I'm sorry," I said, "I didn't get any texts or calls."

"Well, I want a hat. So if the camp store opens, please buy one for me. Now I'm going to go back up the hill to make sure your daughter is still doing ok."

And off he went.

I was stunned.

I turned to my friend who, sitting beside me, had overheard the entire interaction, and had even offered to make him a plate of breakfast.

I said, "He was angry, right?"

I knew he was angry. But I'd known he was angry on other occasions and he'd denied it. Now someone had seen what I've seen for years and I could get her opinion.

"Right?" I asked meekly.

"Yes," she said in a quiet tone.

I tried to dry my tears before anyone could notice I was crying.

Later she told me that the thing that worried her was the impulse to please and cater to him. She'd said that she'd worked a long time in therapy to get over that impulse, but the way he acted was so manipulative and threatening that it triggered a reaction from her that she hadn't experienced for years.

After camp I began keeping a little notebook. A notebook to remind me of hurtful things and the behaviors that continued to happen. I guess it was a sort of anti-gratitude journal. I've written many gratitude journals. Over the years I'd specifically write gratitude journals to try to reframe my thinking toward my husband.

"You're always seeing the bad in me," he'd say. I'd reflect on that and try to do something differently.

"Everything is always my fault and you never need to change anything," he'd say. I'd reflect and try to do something differently.

In 2019, I was beginning to hear the truth in his words. Most of the time, I couldn't think of what I had done wrong in a given situation. I couldn't see things I needed to change, or see how his behaviors should be ok for me to tolerate. I'd even asked him to tell me things to work on. I wanted a partnership to help me grow. I know I am not fully and completely enlightened. He would give me nothing, until he wanted to shift the focus off his own behavior. Maybe it was true that the negativity in our family was primarily his responsibility. If so, is that something I wanted for myself and my kids?

I'm a social worker at heart. I see the worth in everyone and have empathy and compassion for everyone. I'm the kind of person that wonders what that serial killer must have experienced to turn out the way he did. The kind of person that would want to sit with the people on death row with love, light, and healing. It's not a mistake that my husband chose me. It's not a mistake that he targeted my generous, forgiving, merciful, empathic soul. It's people like me that people like him like most. They can twist and turn and make excuses for all of their nasty behaviors, and use our compassion against us. They can do it with such skill that at some point they don't even need to verbalize the excuses. We voice the excuses for them.

This is why I needed to keep the anti-gratitude notebook. I needed reminders that the reasons for his behaviors didn't justify the behaviors. I can be compassionate and also not tolerate abuse. I can allow his painful, snide comments to be painful. I needed it to remind my optimistic soul that gave people two, three or five hundred and seventy-seven chances that no matter how often he said he was going to change, he never did. He never put in the effort. I needed the notebook to help me cling to the truth of my experiences when my dissonant thoughts became confused about what was reality and what wasn't.

I also needed the written reminders because the Prince Charming of our early years would occasionally show back up. He wasn't in full regalia, but he'd offer just enough of a glimpse of the glorious castle life that it kept me on the hook and waiting for more.

He'd hold my hand and I would feel like maybe it could be different this time.

He'd give me a compliment. I'd hope he'd start showing me affection outside of the bedroom again.

Years earlier I'd forgotten my lunch at home. We lived approximately 20 minutes from my work. My husband offered to bring it to me. He dropped off my lunch, and chatted with me and my coworker. My coworker commented on how much I was clearly still in love with him because my eyes were beaming while he was there. He willingly inconvenienced himself for nothing other than to bring me my lunch and it felt so extraordinarily kind. It felt like he truly noticed me and cared about me. It felt like he would do anything to take care of me.

He brought me lunch on a day he had nothing else planned and I felt like he was the world's greatest man ever.

I'd learned to accept scraps as if they were gold and it made me an amnesiac when it came to the abuse.

I'd walked this road for twenty years and I didn't want to walk it anymore. I needed the notebook to remember the abuse. I needed it to keep me focused on whether there was real change. I needed it so I didn't get swept off my feet because he gave me a pumpkin and promised to turn it into a carriage.

Movies had been a continual source of contention in our relationship. Very rarely, probably fewer than five times, did he agree to watch a movie that I chose. He had to approve every movie and he very rarely even considered my suggestions.

Of course it went further than that. Not only did he

refuse to watch anything I wanted to see, he'd mock my television choices, my movies, my books, my music. I'd listen to Christian music and he'd pretend to evangelically raise his hands in the air. I'd tell him to stop and he'd reassure me that he was "just joking."

I cannot count the number of times he said something like, "For such a smart person you sure do watch some stupid stuff." Or, "How can you watch that?" Or, "I can feel myself getting dumber just knowing that show's playing on a tablet next to me."

During the summer of 2019, he felt my exterior hardening and knew he needed to throw me a scrap. He knew I was seeing through the bullshit and he'd have to respond. He suggested we watch movies together at least once a week. He assured me that I would get to pick the movies, too.

I don't remember the first movie I chose, but I remember feeling shamed by him and not feeling like I could relax and enjoy it.

The second movie I chose focused more on his interests than mine.

By the time I was to my third movie, he'd suggested we watch through all the marvel movies together. I'd agreed because I don't mind superhero movies and I just didn't want to put up with the not-so-funny jokes about my choices anymore.

I started seeing the patterns. He'd acquiesce to something I wanted, then make it uncomfortable. I'd give up, and we'd be back where we started, focused on him and his pleasure. Life would be going along, I'd get more frustrated/lonely/hurt/overworked and melt down. He'd promise to change, be kind for a little while and then the tension started to build again.

This pattern is a classic pattern within abusive relationships: tension building, explosion, honeymoon. I knew this, but it never seemed applicable to me because he'd never been physically abusive (aside from the sexual abuse he'd recently started). He'd never outright called me names or overtly abused me as I would have expected in an abusive relationship. And yet, our relationship cycle mirrored that abuse cycle awfully closely.

I'd also been reflecting and reading more about covert narcissism, thanks again to my client and my resonance with the stories and feelings she'd share.

I began to wonder if this was what I was living with. Was I married to a covert narcissist?

I read about the typical narcissistic abuse cycle: idealization, devalue, discard. Very similar to the typical abuse cycle, but slightly different and more nuanced, particularly with covert narcissists.

The idealization phase, or the love bombing, brings targets in. It is a time when narcissists are studying their targets, being overly charming, building the target up, finding their insecurities and directly complimenting those areas, moving fast and furiously and being too good to be true. It is the fairy tale period of the relationship.

The initial idealization phase needs to move fast because

narcissists can't keep this act going for too long. They work quickly to get their target committed and then have their fun devaluing. Overt devaluing is fairly easy to spot: "You stupid slut!" "You can't do anything right!" "You're lucky you trapped me because nobody else would want you."

Covert devaluing, however, is much more subtle. It's the looks and the implications, the subtle blaming and shaming. It's the "I would've thought you'd look around the airplane to make sure we had everything, but whatever" when his hat was lost. It's the "I'm really worried our sons aren't getting enough time from you" or the "You ate all that cheese already?"

When narcissists have sucked all they can from their victim, they leave. Overt discard is literal leaving, cheating, ghosting, etc. Covert discard can be cheating, or playing an exorbitant amount of video games, or not talking to you or existing in the same home but barely acknowledging you exist.

While it's described in phases, narcissists revisit these phases liberally and frequently. If they devalue or discard for too long, they might actually lose their target. They need to pepper in the love bombing. They need to bounce back and forth between pain and joy. It builds neural pathways that keep a person wanting more. The time when the most oxytocin is released (the feel-good bonding chemical) is in anticipation of a loving act. The good times are just as much a part of the abuse as the bad times.

I reflected on my own relationship and the lessons psychologists had learned about intermittent reinforcement. In the 1950s rats were placed in a Skinner box (an experimental box created by psychologist B.F. Skinner). When these rats pressed a button, food would be dispensed. For some rats, food was dispensed every time they pushed the button. For other rats, food was dispensed intermittently. Sometimes they'd push the button and nothing; sometimes they'd push the button and poof! Food! When the scientist entered the extermination phase of the experiment, the levers no longer triggered the release of food. The rats who received food every time the lever was pushed, stopped pushing the button pretty quickly after the food stopped appearing. Those rats that only received food some of the time, kept pushing the lever. Over and over. Nothing came, but they'd been trained to believe that they might get food next time.

I'm not a rat. Other abuse victims are not rats. That said, our brains get wired by our experiences. When my husband would occasionally say something nice or do something sweet or help in an unexpected way, I came to expect that the nice side of him would show up again. In the beginning he needed to give me all sorts of pleasant experiences. With time, he could slowly diminish the amount of kindness he needed to show. But because those kindnesses would occasionally show up, I'd still anticipate them. My brain knew that if I just put up with the shit long enough, the good stuff would come back. And maybe this time it'd come back and stay.

During my awakening, I couldn't grasp and accept all the pieces of narcissism at once. I could see how the cycle played out in my relationship, but certainly it wasn't like that from the start?

Except it was.

The over-the-top romance, the sweetness, poems and carved wooden animals, the hand kisses, compliments and crafted duct taped rings—all of it can be explained by love bombing. The fast paced, pushy future talk, and his immediate drop to his knee to secure my commitment before he moved across the sea? That was love bombing as well. Showing interest in the more challenging kids despite having avoided these kids in past summers? Love bombing. The camp activity he labeled "Lemonade with (insert his name here)" in which, yep, kids signed up to sit in a circle, drink lemonade, and be in his vicinity? Pure outright narcissism that still makes me cringe and wonder how I missed it.

I can't fully explain how jarring and disorienting this realization was. Everything that I thought I'd experienced in the past twenty years had been scripted. All of his side of the courtship and marriage was directed by the same narcissist handbook that every narc seems to read. What I thought was genuine wasn't. The broken and depressed man who I thought just needed care and therapy, was actually a very disturbed man potentially capable of much worse than I ever imagined. What I thought was a loving marriage that just required some work was an abusive relationship that I couldn't fix. And it was calculated from the very beginning.

Aside from how my children have been affected, the most painful consequence of these twenty years has been the deep-seeded distrust of my own perceptions and judgment. I lived a life that was not at all what I thought it was. Just months before autism camp I'd bought artwork that said "And together they built the life they loved." I truly believed it. I knew he wasn't perfect, but no one is. I knew I felt tired, but I was running a business, writing, speaking, parenting and creating a safe environment for an autistic child. I had moments when I loved my life and believed the fairy tale. I was so completely wrong but I am not ashamed of that now. These fuckers are good at what they do. He took my best qualities and warped them into his tools to abuse and manipulate me. I don't feel ashamed, but I do mistrust my judgment. As I write this book, things are improving. But at the time of my awakening, I needed constant reassurance from my closest friends and family. I was an intelligent, empathic therapist who kept pressing the damn lever not realizing that what it dispensed was slowly poisoning me.

I'm a reader and a researcher. If something comes into my life that I don't understand, I don't rest until I do. When I considered homeschooling my children? My bedside was stacked with homeschooling books and resources and various approaches to education. When my daughter was diagnosed with sensory processing disorder? I attended professional training about sensory integration and ways to parent differently. I think my husband is a narcissist? My kindle and podcast libraries look like the archives for the FBI's Behavior Analysis Unit.

Debbie Mirza's work and a guide to abuse provided by Helena Knowlton, *Confusion to Clarity*, provided lists of behaviors I would highlight, re-read and use to recognize examples of the ways these covert abusive tactics were used in my marriage.

Returning to these lists was like keeping someone else's anti-gratitude journal close at hand. It helped me see his behaviors more clearly and reminded me that I wasn't crazy. Every time I read through the lists of psychological abuse tactics, I'd wake up a little more. I'd see past experiences for what they were and my certitude that I was married to a covert narcissist grew stronger. As I saw the past with more clarity, I could identify these stealthy strategies more readily in the moment.

One night he flew off the handle with our daughter. He fauxpologized by saying, "Sorry. I just had an awful night sleep and every time I nearly fell back asleep, you'd snore and wake me back up again." On the surface, and while living in the cloudy muck he'd created over the decades, it would have sounded repentant. With my growing understanding, I could see that he said the word sorry, but he didn't apologize. He justified his behavior and made it something he had no control over. He then blamed me for it because I'd kept him awake all night.

The credit card incident in Houston? He responded decently in the moment, but on at least two occasions following that trip made snide jokes about it. "Are you sure you have your card?" "You're so forgetful lately, it's amazing you haven't lost important things like your car keys or credit cards.

Oh wait. You have." His help came with strings attached and with ridicule.

We were driving back from picking a child up at camp. I said I was really tired and couldn't do the driving. He emphasized what a grand gesture and inconvenience it was for him to drive, and threw in a few strings and a bit of a threat for good measure.

Exaggerated sigh, "Fine. I'll drive, but I was looking forward to reading and listening to my shows. If I'm driving then you'd better sleep."

If I dared ask to buy something for myself, he'd always respond, "Sure. You get that and then I can get this thing over here that I've been wanting." I could never "come out ahead" in his mind. If I got something, he had to get something. "It was only fair." Of course, it'd be fine when random new shirts would show up on his side of the closet or new video games, without reciprocity for me. So long as he felt things were even or he had more, it was fine.

While a t-shirt here or there may not seem like a big deal, money was tight. All of our finances were joint. We had one checking account and one savings account. We'd had to go on a payment plan to pay off credit card debt. We'd bought a new home in 2014 knowing that we'd need to keep a stricter budget to afford it comfortably, but his spending didn't change. And, in fairness, mine didn't change enough either.

He had a sense of entitlement about material things. He wanted nice things, whether we could afford them or not. If I got something, he got something. Gifts given to him needed to be exactly right. Regularly he'd say, "We work so hard, we deserve to splurge a little." Or, when he wanted to be guileful, "Heather, you work so hard, you should go ahead and get that thing you've wanted" and then later in the day justify buying something for himself.

As I said, money was tight. Every month I'd go through the bills and the budget. Every month I'd fill him in on where we stood. Every month he'd complain and in a disgusted voice say, "I thought it was getting better! How are we in this place?" and it was always said with an air of blame. I would stand my ground and say this was a joint venture and I wasn't responsible for the entire financial health of our family. I'd reinforce that he needed to be more involved. I asked him to sit with me and learn how I do it or take it over and do it his own way. He'd say he was bad at math. He'd say he would sit in and do it with me. He'd project hope that it would change, and it never would. Promising a brighter future without intent to change is yet another covert strategy.

We were regularly over the food budget. He shopped for all the groceries and I asked him to start taking cash out, because it seemed too easy for him to go over budget when he just handed over a plastic card. He said he would. He wouldn't. He'd say he would this month. He wouldn't. Month after month he "forgot." Month after month we were over budget.

He seemed to "forget" about a lot of things. Unless they were important to him. It was amazing how specific his memory problems were. This "forgetting" is yet another covert tactic.

We had decided on a budget that included the basics and some "blow money" for each of us to use for ourselves or for those random household expenses that pop up. Aside from some coffees, all of my money went back into the household. Especially during this time when I was choosing which bills to pay or not pay and playing the rob Peter to pay Paul game. His money did not go back into the household. It went to tattoos and tinted windows on his car and t-shirts and anything and everything that served him. This was also the time he justified paying a housecleaner instead of doing the work himself. Of course, that was with household funds, not his extra spending money.

The amount of extra money he had confused me. It seemed if he had extra money for tattoos, we could use that for bills and debt instead.

"I'm just good at saving my monthly money. And it's money we decided we could spend however we wanted. So, go ahead and buy stuff for the house with yours if you want to, I don't have to do the same thing." And he didn't.

There came a time when we literally didn't have the funds to purchase something necessary. I went to him, looking for problem solving. He asked how much we needed, and like an honorable superhero, swooped into a stash in his closet and said, "I can cover it, so long as I get the money back when we can afford it."

He had $1300 squirreled away in an old cigar box in his closet.

My jaw dropped.

After regaining my composure, I said, "where did you get this?"

"I've saved it up over the past few months. I save some of my monthly money. If I have any extra gas money, I save that. Birthday money, Christmas money, you know."

It didn't make sense. He couldn't have been buying all the things he'd been buying and save $1300 in a few months. I asked what he planned to do with it. He said get things for himself. I reminded him that we can't pay bills and maybe it should go to help us be $1300 more financially stable. He said it was his money. I asked if I could throw a few bucks in every once in a while, and we could use it for a vacation fund or something. He said I could put money in, but that he wanted final say on how the money was spent.

For weeks I contemplated this and ran the numbers in my head. It simply didn't add up. There was no reasonable way he could save that amount of money in that short of time.

The groceries! I pulled out an old grocery bag that still had the receipt in it. Sure enough, the receipt showed cash had been withdrawn. Groceries were bought and a near equal amount of cash was withdrawn. He literally stole money from his family to buy himself shit. This became even more evident after we separated. For a few months we nested, meaning the kids stayed in the family home and he and I would go back and forth. He was still buying the groceries. Every time I went to the fridge, there was maybe $50 worth of food to work with, and yet the same over-budget amounts continued to be "spent" at the grocery store from our joint account every week.

The year leading up to the separation was dizzying. The more I saw the more I could see. Every new realization sparked reflection on other events. I'd scratched the surface of a tiny anthill and fallen into Alice's pit to wonderland. And the deeper down the hole I swirled, the more I recognized how the previous twenty years had truly destroyed me.

I'd grown soul weary. There's tired. Then there's exhausted. Weary. And then there's *soul* weary. I literally didn't know how I put one foot in front of the other anymore. I didn't have a choice to stop, but I didn't feel like I could keep going. I pushed and pushed, but felt like I went nowhere. Tears were more common than smiles. Overwhelm more common than peace. We worked opposite schedules, so I thought my loneliness stemmed from not seeing my spouse, until I realized I felt loneliest when he was home with me. I'd been slowly coming back to myself, slowly knowing who I was again outside of work and parenting. And I'd been slowly recognizing the depth to which my anxiety correlated to his presence. The more I learned, the more I realized my destruction came at his hands. And the more I recognized him in the narcissism books, the more I realized my destruction could have been his goal from the beginning.

As I've mentioned, he seemed supportive in many ways. He'd brag about my work. He wouldn't hesitate when I needed to travel or take time away to write. He seemingly supported all of my crazy ideas and endeavors. I came to realize these moments of pride were not about me at all. He felt important by association. He didn't say, "Heather did so and so." He said, "My wife did such and such." The first time he saw me speak publicly he said, "Wow. I knew you'd do great, but that was amazing. And the whole time I kept thinking, 'I get to go home with her.'" He couldn't let it be just about me. He had to lay claim and associate himself with whatever successes I had.

I'd been invited to give a spotlight talk at a large regional conference. It was in the style of a Ted Talk, so I had 18 minutes to share an engaging, personalized, but thought-provoking message. It was the first really big talk I'd given. Nervous, anxious, nauseous all pretty much sum up how I felt as the time grew closer.

About two weeks prior to this conference I had been diagnosed with bronchitis. My voice hung on by a thread as I started speaking, but about halfway through it gave out just a little and I started coughing. I couldn't find any water on the stage, so my ever so thoughtful husband brought up a bottle of water to me. I thanked him. People clapped. End of story.

Except it wasn't. Part of the gig included attending a cocktail hour after the talks. Naturally, people came up to me to congratulate me, or thank me, or ask questions. Every single time someone talked to me, he mentioned he was the guy with the water bottle. He'd make a joke, put on his charming voice, keep it light-hearted. At the time I thought it was endearing. I'm actually very introverted and while I'm capable of chit chat and socializing, it isn't my favorite way to spend my time. It drains my energy and brain power. Him chipping in to the conversation felt like maybe he was taking care of me a little. Taking the burden of conversing off my shoulders. Every time that particular conference came up in conversation in the years to follow, he mentioned the water bottle and his grand gesture. It wasn't about taking care of me; it was about making sure the spotlight shone on him too.

All of my successes had to be about him. Funnily enough, a few years later we spoke together and something I said resonated with the crowd, so they applauded. His response? "You can applaud for me too, you know." To those of us who weren't in the know, it came off as a charming joke. To those of us who understood narcissism, it came off as a desperate inability to simply let someone else be appreciated.

Subtly gathering praise is the covert narc's favorite game time play. It allows space for plausible deniability. "I was simply making a joke. I don't care if people recognize me or not." Their overt cousins do not care what others think. They will loudly proclaim they are the best speakers to walk this planet. The covert narcissist, however, prefers mindfuckery. He prefers to manipulate people into giving him praise and prefers to come across as the good guy.

Prior to the event, my husband had been looking for an example of supportive humor that he'd received from a mutual friend. He scrolled back through their texts and decided none of our friend's comments were good enough, so he chose to highlight one of his own jokes. Not being an overt narcissist or wanting to come across as a self-aggrandizing jackass, he attributed the joke to our friend. During the talk, it did get laughter from the crowd. Knowing that it was his own joke he was able to absorb that laughter as personal adoration, all while the crowd believed they were laughing at his friend's humor.

After speaking with this friend about my thoughts toward the end of 2019, she told her mom, who'd also known us both. My friend said, "I think he's a narcissist." Her mom said, "Oh yeah. I know that. He's way too flashy and clearly just rides on Heather's coattails."

As I continued to unwrap the layers, I realized that bogarting the spotlight wasn't his only motivation. He also enjoyed the life in which I worked hard and he didn't. If ever I tried to convey my soul weariness to him, he'd tell me I chose it. Absolutely no compassion or empathy given. He'd even said it wasn't fair for him do extra work around the house just because I chose to work so much. Other times he'd cut me off, groan, and say, "Yeah, yeah, I know you're tired. I am too."

On paper he could claim he supported my endeavors, but in reality, he supported me only insofar as he wasn't inconvenienced or expected to be loving about it.

These are all covert manipulation and narcissistic traits. Most gain for the least amount of effort. Gain attention, whether pleasant or unpleasant, for the least energy expended.

One thing motivates a narcissist: supply. Many theories

exist as to how narcissists come to be, but all theories identify that despite their sometimes grandiose presentations of themselves, they actually lack a true sense of self. They have no identity separate from their interactions with others. At first this didn't seem to apply to the man I married, but then I realized, he'd even verbalized his lack of sense of self to me. He'd repeatedly said he didn't know how to describe himself. Other than his profession, he had no true interests. He played video games. He read. But there was no strong sense of self and identity.

Because narcissists don't have an innate sense of self, they strive constantly to find proof that they exist and that they can influence the world. They accomplish this by manipulating others. They seek positive attention and adoration. When others are noticing them, they feel influential. They also seek negative attention and emotional reactivity. They know that if other people get angry, or sad, or terrified because of their actions, then they have influence and exist. The emotional reactions of people in their midst gives narcissists life. Everything they do is to get a reaction.

Like everything related to humans, narcissism exists on a spectrum. The more malicious the narcissist, the more supply they receive from fucking up other people's lives. Pleasant reactions and emotions give the narc some supply, but negative reactions and emotions *really* fill their gas tank.

I couldn't completely see the intentionality or maliciousness right away. I was wrapping my mind around the fact that my whole marriage had been tearing me down. As I grew soul weary, he grew more powerful. Could that be intentional? That seemed difficult to grasp. Surely it was just behavior learned somewhere. Surely, he wasn't malignant.

In August of 2019, my mom retired and had one of those birthdays with a zero at the end. To celebrate, she rented a house on an island in Wisconsin and hosted her children and grandchildren for a weekend of family time. This place reminded me of the resort from *Dirty Dancing*—horseshoes and hiking trails and hammocks and kayaks. Old fashioned fun.

My husband saw our sleeping quarters and complained. He had a negative energy the whole weekend. He complained that the bed wasn't big enough, that there wasn't enough space, that our autistic daughter couldn't handle it, that he should just take her home now before the meltdowns, etc. To accommodate him, I slept on a mattress on the floor. He also complained about the food. The amount of food my mom brought was never sufficient or considerate enough for him. He'd make snide comments in front of the kids. He'd say things like, "We'd better eat before we get there because who knows if there'll be anything we like."

I asked for gratitude. I asked for appreciation. He knew no other way than to be entitled and judgmental.

The weekend was truly beautiful. I'd been practicing differentiation and had learned to mostly shut him out.

There is one incident from that weekend that is seared in my mind, however. Mom was treating us all to one dinner in the main restaurant. We were on an island, so the restaurant was the only option aside from cooking in the rental home.

I'd come back from a hike and told him what time we were meeting at the restaurant.

He said, "Okay. Do they have mashed potatoes and food your daughter will eat?"

I said, "I don't know, but I'm sure we'll find something."

"You should go talk to the kitchen and make sure they'll be able to make mashed potatoes."

"I'm sure we'll find something for her. We always find something. It should be fine."

He closed the distance. His body about six inches away from mine and his face towering over me, he gave the look. But not just the look. The most hate-filled, spiteful, disgusted, silently raging look I've ever seen. He did his sniff and nose wrinkle thing. He glared down at me and with clenched jaw said in a slow, menacing voice, "Let me rephrase this for you. You *will* go talk to the kitchen and make sure there are mashed potatoes so your *autistic* daughter has something to eat for dinner."

He sneered, mumbled "fucking hell" with a disgusted shake of his head, and walked away.

I stood, tears in my eyes, heart racing, and paralyzed with fear.

After a moment I took a breath and walked out of the house. I went to the kitchen and did as I was told.

I didn't go to the kitchen because I wanted to or thought

it was necessary. I went to the kitchen because the consequences if I didn't terrified me. This was abuse.

It was in that moment that I could truly label it. I wasn't living with narcissism lite or just a messed-up man. I was living with an abuser, who bullied and threatened to get his way. Who forced me to do all the work. Who had no empathy or compassion. Who enjoyed the power and coercive control he'd fostered through the years. He did not love me. No one who loved me could treat me that way. He did not love me. He wasn't capable of loving anyone.

After that weekend I doubled down on my efforts to understand narcissism and covert abuse. I'd learned I couldn't trust my own experiences, so I started asking family and friends if they saw it too. I needed confirmation from others.

I first talked to my best friend who was at camp with us. Yes. He's not a good man. She always felt stupid around him and didn't know why. She read more about covert narcissism and confirmed it described him in detail.

I talked to my mom. I asked what she thought of my husband. She was thrown off guard and didn't really know what to say. After I explained more about what I had been identifying, she said, "Well, I could see that. I've always gotten along with him, but yeah, as I think about it, I don't really like the way he talks to your daughter." She said she hoped we could work it out.

I was a bit dejected, but I also knew my mom would be supportive of me no matter what. A few days later she told me she'd had time to think about it, and she definitely saw my reactions to him and didn't like the way I looked shut down.

I talked to my brother. After I stumbled around with my words for a while, he said, "Are you asking if I think he's emotionally manipulative? Yes. Without a doubt. There's even been a few times I've nearly taken him outside to talk to him and set him straight after he said some things to my wife and kids."

I received the validation I needed and kept moving forward.

I'd concluded he was a covert narcissist. I'd concluded that my kids were not living the life they deserved. I concluded that I was not living the life I deserved. And I concluded I needed to tell him.

Talking to him wasn't the best conclusion I'd ever drawn. The literature recommends NOT having this conversation if there's a narcissist in your life. At best, they'll deny or play along and use it as another chance to love bomb and promise to change. At worst, they'll feel threatened, feel narcissistic injury, and lash out in rage.

My narc was going to be different though. He didn't know he was a narcissist and if he only knew then he'd change his behaviors. He didn't want to hurt me or the kids; he'd said so on numerous occasions. The fact that he lied about practically everything made no difference in this situation. He wanted to change and despite twenty years of trying, we hadn't figured out what needed to change. I finally had the answer and it would be different.

That's how I felt at the time. The confusion and cognitive dissonance was all encompassing. I couldn't give up hope. I believed that the "real" him was the love bombing Prince Charming. The other, cruel parts of him were anomalies. They could be fixed. I cannot overstate how difficult it was to fully accept that the man I spent half my life with never loved me. Logically, it feels like once I knew, I should have known. But the full, guttural reality isn't revealed with one big parting of the theatrical curtain. It falls aside slowly, like the stage is filled with hundreds of 3rd graders pushing the curtain to reveal tiny little glimpses of what lies ahead. It's those videos of colorblind people putting on color spectrum glasses for the first time. No one ever just puts them on and leaves them there. They put them on, slide them off, put them on, slide them off, comparing the vision they have always known with the vision of the world that they are seeing for the first time.

I was slipping the glasses on and off. And I was giving him all the benefits of the doubt. That's who I am. That's what I do. That's why I was targeted by a covert narcissist.

Ironically, I spoke with him after church. The kids went off to do their own things. He was sitting on the porch reading. I joined him and asked to talk.

I told him I thought he's a narcissist. I told him all the things I'd seen in his relationships with the kids. I'd told him that something needed to change. I gave him my highlighted list of all the covert manipulation tactics he'd used.

He sat stunned. Not surprised or shocked or worried,

but quiet and trying to figure out how to talk himself out of this one.

"Gaslighting?" He said. "I don't gaslight. Wait, I suppose that could have just been me gaslighting." There it was—his anti-laugh.

"When have I ever played the victim?" he asked.

"After the affair and we'd moved back here? I was angry when I'd found out you'd still been in communication with her. I was outside crying about how much I'd lost. You said that you lost things too. You said that you lost your best friend because of it."

"I said that? Shit. That's pretty shitty.".

There was no apologizing, no real remorse. He stated a fact. His behavior was shitty.

He said he'd read about it. He said he'd think about it. I suggested he speak to his mentor and see what he thinks.

He bought a couple of books on Kindle that very day and read a couple of pages. Our accounts were connected and it tells you how much of the book has been read across devices. He stopped after those couple of pages.

A week later he went for drinks with his mentor and said he talked to him about it and he thought it was just anxiety. He never talked about this mentor or went for drinks with him again.

I told him something needed to change and he needed to see a therapist. I told him I'd be seeing a therapist. He suggested couples counseling. Couples counseling is contraindicated for couples experiencing narcissistic abuse. The narcissist doesn't want to change and will manipulate sessions to look like the good guy. They will then use any vulnerabilities the victim shares against them. I told him I wanted to do individual therapy first. He agreed.

He told me his therapist thinks he just has severe anxiety. I thought of the airplane and his denial of anxiety.

I said it doesn't really matter what it is called, it's abusive and needs to stop.

He bought a board game.

I love board games, as do my kids. I grew up playing cards most weekends with my family and regularly played cards with my high school friends. He made one attempt while we were engaged to learn a card game and then never tried again. I hadn't played cards for the entire duration of our marriage. He said he liked trivia games. So I bought some. He wouldn't play. His kids would ask to play a board game. He'd grumble and say no or find a way to ruin the game with a piss poor attitude and belittling jokes. He complained about not having enough sex and I said, connect with me, give me time and conversation, play a board game with me. He didn't.

And then he knew shit was getting real. He knew he needed to hoover me back or risk his main supply walking out of his life. So he bought a board game. We played it once. The night he bought it. I knew that was going to be the one and only time we'd play it. I was right.

He came to me and said, "I forgot I have a call I have to be on tomorrow. I think I'll just do my check-in at the beginning and then leave the phone on mute in my car while I run these errands."

I said, "Or, you could tell them you have a scheduling conflict and that you'll only be able to attend the first twenty minutes."

"Oh, yeah, that's what I'll do."

"I mean, seriously, just be honest," I said.

"Hmm. Yeah. That's probably why I talked to you about it," he said.

"Huh?"

"Because you're my moral compass. If I'm going to change and recognize what I'm doing, I need your help."

I didn't know how to process this conversation. First of all, I was learning that I am not responsible for his ethics, morals or what choices he makes. Second of all, I don't want to be the angel of the household from Victorian time, charged with keeping everyone holy. Thirdly, he couldn't decide just to be honest without me telling him not to lie? That's preschool skills. Was this what I wanted? Most narcissists don't change or can't change. The best bet is to go no contact. I wasn't ready to completely throw in the towel, but if I stayed and he couldn't change, is this what my life would be? Living as his moral compass that he sometimes would listen to and sometimes wouldn't?

I did some more reading. I read *In Sheep's Clothing* by George K. Simon. In it he argues that some people are simply character disturbed. He argues that all manipulative behavior is intentional, though not always conscious.

I read works by a self-proclaimed narcissist. He wrote about the tactics of manipulation through the mindset of a malignant narcissist. It was chilling. And both of these books had me rethinking my perspectives on my spouse's version of narcissism. Perhaps he was more malignant than I thought.

The husband, kids and I were going to a holiday breakfast event. It was a fundraiser. They didn't have gluten free pancakes. We'd already bought the tickets and my husband asked if we could get a refund because my daughter and I wouldn't be able to eat anything, so we'd only be doing the activities. She looked at him blankly and said, "It's a fundraiser and in order to go inside for the activities they need to have a ticket." He chastised her, anti-laughed, shook his head in a disgusted, superior way and walked in.

When I told my friend about this, she asked, "Are you sure it isn't intentional? I think he knows what he's doing and he's doing it on purpose to make people feel small and get what he wants."

The last few months of 2019 were less about whether or not I was living with a covert narcissist. I knew I was. Instead, I was contemplating whether I wanted to continue living with a narcissist.

He'd made some gestures, but I'd known enough about the cycle now to know he was love bombing and it wouldn't last. It didn't. The look returned. The chiding and chastising continued. He went back to life as usual, expecting that this was like any other time over the past two decades. Previously he could smooth things over for a quick minute and I'd forget about it.

It wasn't like all those times. I had the names for it now. I knew what I was living with now. I wasn't sure if recovery was possible. I didn't know if he was evil or didn't know any better. Regardless of the answer to that, I wasn't sure if I wanted to put up with it anymore.

I'd been reading that I needed to listen to my body. So I did.

I meditated and listened.

I puttered around the house and listened.

I listened as I prayed and cried all over the darkened sanctuary stairs.

I listened as I tensed when I heard his garage door open.

I listened as I felt nauseous pulling into the driveway.

I listened as I lay in bed next to him, stiff, filled with anxiety and tension, willing myself not to fall asleep as I clung to the piping on the mattress and tears trickled across my face.

I don't know why it hit me when it did. I was sitting alone in my bed and for some reason it finally connected. I suppose the curtain had opened a little further and I saw that his actions might not all be ignorant. I saw that he was exerting control and this realization was the next logical step.

I took out my phone and googled "definition of marital rape."

He had been raping me.

But no. He couldn't have been raping me. He's not a rapist.

I read the definition again.

He had been raping me.

But I didn't *feel* like a sexual assault survivor. There wasn't violent force or threats or weapons. I wasn't having nightmares and flashbacks.

I read the state law. Weapons, violence or threats do not have to be present for it to be rape. "Of course not," the logical part of me said. "That woman behind the dumpster had passed out. Her rapist didn't need to use anything to intimidate her. Children are raped regularly without threats, violence or weapons. You counsel people regularly that abuse and sexual assault don't look like Hollywood portrays them."

The other part of me argued that he had to love me. He'd said he was trying to pleasure me.

"Heather, you didn't want it. You didn't consent," my logical mind countered.

I read the law again. I was asleep and could not give consent. He engaged in sexual contact without consent.

I'd been raped.

Multiple times.

By my husband.

But why? Why would he do that if it wasn't to please me? He got nothing out of it. He didn't climax. His penis stayed in his pants.

Because rape is about power and control, not sexual gratification. It has nothing to do with sex. It has everything to do with claiming control over someone, with making the victim feel small and unsafe, with feeling powerful.

No sexual pleasure needed when the goal was to know that no matter my accomplishments, status, or influence, no matter the confidence and strength I was gaining, he still dominated me. He owned me. He proved to himself, and to me, that everything I have and all that I was belonged to him.

Of course it was rape.

I was raped.

Repeatedly.

By my husband.

I had to keep saying it. Out loud even.

I was shocked and stunned and the curtain opened and all the pieces fell into place.

I could finally acknowledge why my body froze, why I cringed when he touched me, why I couldn't look him in the eye.

He was a rapist.

I was his victim.

Like the good communicator I am, I, of course, needed to talk to him about it. I'm not sure what I hoped to achieve through this conversation. Maybe some accountability or acknowledgement. Maybe I simply needed to voice my awakened understanding.

He came home and I confronted him. I don't remember how I brought it up. I remember him standing in silence with a shocked look on his face. I remember saying, through tears, "You raped me!" I remember his response clearly: "I'm sorry that happened to you."

I threw my hands up and walked away.

After this confrontation I told him I didn't feel safe sleeping in the same bed as him. He said, "It's not like I'm going to hurt you or anything." When I persisted, he did offer to sleep in the guest room.

I told him I needed him to stay there every night until I could deal with this, and he agreed.

One night I felt particularly unsafe and I locked the door. He came up in the morning to get ready for work and found the door locked. I let him in. He shook his head, gave me a scathing look, and said, "Sheesh. Seriously? You need to lock the door?" I ignored his minimization of my needs and read in bed until he left for work.

We were talking with a friend and somehow the conversation turned toward sexual assault and rape culture. He began speaking like a big, progressive, defender of women's rights, and I just couldn't. I couldn't sit there and listen to the bullshit he was spewing knowing that he was a perpetrator. I left the room abruptly. I had confided in my friend about the rapes and she came and knocked on the door and said, "I'm so sorry. I didn't even think about it. He left, so come out when you're ready."

When trauma is triggered it is intense. Emotions and physical sensations hijack the body and brain. It doesn't just fade after a few minutes. I spent the rest of the day feeling anxious, on edge, and afraid to go home. I parked in a nearby lot and sobbed for about fifteen minutes before I felt courageous enough to drive down my driveway.

It was a late night for me, so the kids were already in bed, and I was hoping he was asleep already too. He was asleep. He was sleeping in the master bed just a few days after he agreed to sleep downstairs. I tipped over the edge. I nearly threw up in the bathroom. I paced and sobbed and didn't know what to do.

I supposed I had three options. I could wake him up and make him move. I could sleep downstairs in the guest room. I could sleep in the bed next to my rapist.

I ruled out the third option immediately. And pretty quickly also ruled out option number two. Narcissists are notorious boundary breakers. They will tiptoe, push, lean over, and crash through the lines any of their victims set. If this boundary crossing is allowed even one time, they will push farther the next. I knew that if I let him sleep in this bed for even one night, he would never leave it again.

So I pushed on his leg. And through hiccupped sobs shouted his name.

He woke bleary eyed and with disgust said, "Jesus fucking Christ! What the hell is going on?"

"You need to move downstairs," I said with tears and wheezy gasps as punctuation.

"Seriously?" he asked with ridicule.

"Yes."

He grumbled softly enough to pretend he was saying it under his breath, but loudly enough that it was clear he wanted me to hear it, "I can't even sleep in my own bed for one night. My god this is ridiculous. I'm exhausted, but nope! My bed isn't allowed." He grabbed his pillow and slammed the door behind him.

I locked it and sobbed myself to sleep.

That night was never spoken of again.

I knew I needed a separation to figure out what I wanted. I couldn't determine my future sleeping in the same bed or home as my rapist. My prayers and meditations were filled with the phrase, "be free," and I decided to listen.

PART 3

Freedom

I am writing these words nearly four years free. I just wrote the words about being sexually assaulted. As I'm beginning this section, I am doubting my trauma. Maybe I'm making a bigger deal out of this than it is. Maybe I'm not portraying my story in a fair way. Maybe my perceptions were skewed.

I am nearly four years "free" and yet I'm not completely free. I live with real, gentle, caring, passionate, selfless love every day from a beautiful soul who loves me because of who I am. He challenges me and supports me and loves my curves. I now know what it means to be truly loved. It feels uplifting and protective and sweet and hot and calming and empowering and nothing, *nothing* like my first marriage. Yet, there are still deeply rooted beliefs and cognitive vultures picking at my brain and distorting my self-trust. My ex successfully and intentionally planted niggling thoughts deep inside the marrow of my bones. They kept me from knowing the truth of our relationship and they keep me from trusting my perceptions.

I am nearly four years "free," with very little contact with him, and yet I'm not completely free. I am free enough that I can share my experience in the hopes that victims might be able to see more clearly and find peace. I am free enough to risk becoming public when for twenty years it felt unsafe to reveal the family secrets. Despite this freedom, confusion binds my brain and uncertainty shackles my heart. Cognitive dissonance is real and confusing and the hallmark of covert abuse.

I am four years free and I still have times I can't see it clearly. When you live in the middle of the conditioning and mindfuckery, amid the kind behaviors and awful behaviors, and sweetness and hatreds whirl around you daily, you can't see it. I couldn't see it. She doesn't leave because she doesn't know. He tolerates it because he doesn't know there's a partner out there who he won't have to tolerate.

It has nothing to do with intelligence or education. In fact, the beautiful traits that go with intelligence often make a person a perfect target. It has nothing to do with gullibility or any failing on the victims' part. Abusers abuse. Narcissists manipulate. Covert narcissistic abusers create neural pathways in their victims' brains that take years to rewire and that hide the reality of their situation. They carve deep chasms in their victims' souls like the Colorado river created the Grand Canyon.

These neural pathways and soul disintegrations should have nothing to do with our discussion about people leaving abusive situations or not. The question shouldn't be, "Why doesn't she leave?" Asking that question focuses on the victim. Most often, *she* was loving as decent humans are meant to love and did nothing wrong. Why doesn't she leave? *Why does he abuse?* When we focus on victim behaviors, we take the focus off abuser behaviors. We subtly blame the victim because she just put up with it and didn't get out. The perpetrator gets let off the hook, as though once the victim leaves the abuser isn't going to find a new victim to abuse and deplete.

The absolute most dangerous time for an abused person is when they are leaving. An angry narcissist is one thing. An angry narcissist who feels he's losing control and his supply is potentially deadly. Abusers who have previously refrained from physical abuse can become physically assaultive as their partner leaves. Threats, violence, fear tactics, financial abuse, stalking, all intermingled with hoovering, become more desperate as the victim grows stronger and moves further out of the abuser's grasp. I've counseled many women who have stayed *because* they knew their abuser would follow them and become fatally aggressive.

Thankfully, physical aggression has not been a part of my story. Even so, I had an ever-present awareness that it could, and the abuse behaviors certainly ramped up as I sought my freedom and set my boundaries.

I let him know I needed a separation. I said I wanted it to be at least three months. We agreed to wait until after Christmas so the kids wouldn't have the disintegration of their parents' marriage forever linked with the holidays.

"My parents are going to be coming over Christmas. I'm not going to be able to keep sleeping in the guest bed," he said.

I knew this was coming. I told him we'd just have to stay in the same bedroom again while they were here and then he could move back downstairs.

I asked him if we were going to tell his parents while they were here. I said they'd probably appreciate being told in person.

He said he didn't want to.

For my kids, I pretended that nausea and anxious tension didn't overwhelm my body whenever I sat in a room with their father. I can feel it now, that gagging, throat closed and chest heavy feeling I had when near this man.

That Christmas brings up a few blurry memories and nothing more.

We were lying in bed next to each other. He took up his half of the bed and I scooted as far to the edge as I could without falling off. I knew I needed a separation, but didn't yet know how permanent I wanted that separation to be. I would try to make conversation or look for positive times to see if anything worth saving existed. I told him that the day had been pleasant. We talked a bit. He then told me I should go put on some lingerie because he had a dream about me in it the previous night.

I froze.

I cried.

I felt like I should be the good wife and do as he said. And I felt gross that I felt like I should be the good wife and do as he said. I had never considered my role as spouse in such terms.

No way in hell did I want to be naked next to him. I told him it was unfair to put me in that position. He said something about not meaning to put me in that position, "Just don't do it, it's fine," he said and rolled his back to me.

I cried the first time my new man held me. Not until his arms wrapped around me and held me close did I realize that I'd never actually been held in such a protective and loving way. After twenty years with the other guy, I had grown skilled at hiding my tears, so my new man didn't know I'd cried until I told him later. I just told him I liked the way he held me with intention. He held me tighter and kissed my forehead.

When our body enters into starvation mode, usually after one to two days without food, it stops creating the hormone that makes us feel hungry. Our bodies are designed to be kind to us. In case of food shortage, it lessens the desire for food to ease our suffering. I had grown so accustomed to my husband's back and so starved for affection and physical touch that I no longer recognized my suffering.

The Christmas festivities came and went. The parent visit came and went. The time had come to discuss the logistics of the separation. He plead his case to stop the separation. I stood steadfast, with my stomach in knots and my heart crushing through my ribs. Holding boundaries when they've been ignored and stomped on feels so difficult and scary.

I wanted to nest.

He said he didn't have anywhere to go and that he could just stay in the basement on his days off.

I said I wasn't comfortable with that.

He said, "What do you want me to do? Sleep in a hotel?!" His voice was rising. I wanted to ask him to please not yell, but I'd been trained out of doing that years before. Anytime I'd mentioned that he was yelling, he would deny it and say he was just speaking loudly. I was being too sensitive.

Instead of asking him not to yell, I said, "We don't have the money for you to stay in a hotel multiple nights a week for three months."

Gleefully he responded, "I know. Which is why I suggested the basement."

"I'm not comfortable with you in the basement and I think it would be confusing for the kids. We're nesting to make it easier for the kids, not to confuse them."

"Well I don't have anywhere else to stay. I left all my family over in England when I moved here to marry you." He threw his hands up in the air as though no solution existed, walked away and left the problem for me to fix, as usual.

I told my friends about this. I told them I didn't know how to get the separation I needed because he didn't have anywhere to go.

My friends reminded me that he's a grown ass man and it's his own job to find a place to stay.

My friends reminded me that it isn't my fault he has no one to turn to. He moved to the US nearly twenty years ago, which is plenty of time to build relationships. They reminded me that even if my family wasn't available, I've got other options with friends. They also reminded me that not being able to maintain long term friendships is a sign of narcissism.

We owned the house together, so the option to completely throw him out didn't exist. I stuck to my boundaries and desire for nesting and helped him brainstorm possibilities. Ultimately, he found a place, we settled on a schedule and chose to begin nesting the end of January. It was time to tell the kids.

When leaving a narcissist, one of their tried and true strategies is to gather a group of supporters around them and smear your name and reputation as much as possible. Some theorists call these supporters the narcissist's flying monkeys; some call them lieutenants. The narcs especially enjoy bad-mouthing you in front of the children and many successfully turn their kids against the victimized parent, at least temporarily. Knowing this, I insisted we tell the children together. I knew he already was talking badly about me to them. He had done so from the time they were old enough to have their own opinions. No way was I going to let him lay the blame on me.

We told them that our marriage wasn't working well anymore and we needed space to figure out how to both be happy. We told them that both of us loved them, that no one was to blame and that no matter what happened—whether we stay husband and wife or not—that the five of us will always be a family. After talking through the schedule, the kids all recognized that not much would actually change for them. Given our work schedules and the way we'd divided parenting duties, the only days that would be different were Sundays.

By the end of January 2020 our nesting began. It was difficult. It was exhausting. But it kept the changes as slight as possible for my kids and they did well with this step of the change. Petty things would happen in my absence from the home. Some of my cash would disappear, If I didn't have time to do the dishes before I left for work, I'd come back from my weekend and those dishes would still be sitting next to the sink. I felt annoyed, but I tried to block it out.

I took the time to love my kids well and to reflect on what I needed and how I felt to be outside of his energy for an extended period of time. I read about narcissism and psychological manipulation. I reflected more on the past and ways in which I now saw all those events differently. I grieved. I rested.

As I've said, one of the hardest parts was accepting that it wasn't real from the beginning. Sure, it became bad, but it wasn't bad from the beginning, right? There's no way all that sweet stuff at the start was just a rouse, part of a plan. Except, everything else matched. If I'm to believe that he's a narcissist, and the steps in the beginning of our relationship paralleled the idealization phase of other manipulative relationships... One of his favorite phrases was, if it looks like a horse and sounds like a horse and acts like a horse, the logical conclusion is that it's a horse. I couldn't decide he's a part time narcissist. He either is a narcissist or he isn't.

In the same vein, I couldn't decide he was a part time liar. He lied about everything. Whether he'd sent cards to his family. Why he was late. What he did with the kids. Where the money went. Where the shirts came from. And yet, I'd find myself wanting to believe him. Wanting to trust him. So much so that I'd forget he was a liar until he reminded me again.

He'd say he was running late for some reason or another. I'd call him on it. He'd come up with some other excuse, one that sometimes even directly contradicted the first excuse. When I said it sounded like he just didn't want to come to the thing he was running late for, he'd tell me I always assumed the worst of him and never gave him the benefit of the doubt. I suppose this was true. After twenty years of assuming the best and giving him so many chances, my doubt benefits had been used up long ago.

During the nesting, he'd vacillate between trying to trigger nostalgia, sympathy and fear in me. On one occasion, he called to tell me that our oldest had started to read one of his favorite books—a book that he'd given to me early in our relationship. He said our son had noticed the inscription and said something to him. He said he'd started crying when he read the sweet words he'd written. I said ok.

Later in the day I sat with my oldest and mentioned that dad said he was reading the book again. He had a confused expression, but I went on and asked what motivated him to read it and how'd he like it. He told me he hadn't thought about that book for ages and definitely wasn't reading it now. I covered for his dad and said I must have misheard, but we both know I'd just caught him in another lie. An unnecessary lie. A lie that served absolutely no purpose. He could have said he saw the book and read the inscription. He could have said he was thinking about it. He could have not called at all and given me the space I repeatedly asked for.

If he lied about that and other things, how could I possibly decipher when he told the truth. Instead of trying, I decided to believe him. Believe that he lied. All the time. I could trust absolutely nothing he said.

I learned to employ a technique called grey stoning. It's actually called gray rocking, but I often confuse the name and call it grey stoning instead. Remembering that narcissists derive their sense of self and pleasure by creating reactions from their supply, the goal becomes to give them no reactions. Do not give them what they want. Be a grey stone. Flat, steady, unmoving. Emotions will arise, but they stay tucked inside the grey stone exterior to be released with friends or in writing or when you're hiking alone in the woods.

Every time he tried his tricks, I embodied the grey stone. On that particular occasion when he felt the need to remind me of the sweet things he'd written back in the days when he still paid attention to me and love bombed me, I successfully grey stoned. I said ok. Interesting that the phrase which hooked me into the marriage became the phrase that released those hooks, too.

In February of 2020, I took a weekend alone on the beach. Me, the ocean, a spa day and nothing but my introspection.

I knew I needed quiet around me to bring stillness within. The lack of responsibility and noise of daily life allowed me to be honest with myself and the universe. I took my wedding ring off when I checked into the condo and left it off the entire weekend. I wanted to know what it would feel like without the visual reminder of what life had been.

I cried. I prayed. I listened. I meditated. I walked and I collected shells.

I believe beings that exist beyond our human awareness leave us signs. Especially when we ask for them. This was a weekend devoted to asking for direction, healing, and finding my security.

I've never had luck finding good shells. Maybe I wasn't on the right beaches or maybe I have been too enamored by the horizon and the endless waves of the ocean kissing both the sky and sand. Whatever the reason, I have never had luck finding good shells. Stumbling upon a three inch, intact conch shell, therefore, filled me with joy and curiosity. Returning to the condo I grabbed my prize shell and my phone. The spiritual symbolism of the conch shell varies, but in general, they are seen as symbols of regeneration, fresh starts and cleansing negative, oppressive, evil energy from the environment.

I sat with this. Was this my answer? I'm pretty sure I'd already known what my answer needed to be. How could I possibly stay married to this man now that I have seen behind the mask and acknowledged what he is? I took, and still take, marriage vows very seriously. I married for eternity. I'd said so many times that I didn't believe in divorce. I thought it was an easy out. I thought marriage is hard work and we've become a society that runs from hard work.

I'd said I didn't believe in divorce so frequently that he threw it in my fac when I asked for a separation. Sarcastic, anti-laugh, angry eyes. "I thought you didn't believe in divorce," he spat.

My therapist had reminded me that divorce in Jesus times was actually frowned upon because it would leave the woman neglected, without safety, abused and alone. Women couldn't choose to divorce, only men. Women couldn't work, only men. Women followed their patriarchal families, first their father's and then their spouse's. Women couldn't remarry. If a man chose to divorce a woman, he chose to make the woman an outcast destined to suffer until her death. My therapist said God isn't against divorce. God is against suffering. In particular, God is against the suffering of vulnerable people.

I always advocated for people to leave abusive situations. I did not believe the covenant of marriage sanctified abuse. I did not believe women had to answer to men. But, ingrained in me were the teachings that the righteous woman is loyal, faithful, patient, kind, selfless. Selfless. Without a self. Is that really what we're called to be? I cannot imagine that any divine spirit created women to sacrifice to the point that we have no self and no identity. Yet, that's what I'd been living into. Not consciously, but fully. I downplayed my accomplishments and gave credit to him even though he frequently made my work more difficult and my parenting more heartbreaking. I made decisions out of anxiety and fear rather than out of the knowing of my soul.

In that condo, it was with renewed clarity that I understood that I couldn't be responsible for him, nor was I ever responsible for him. I knew that divorce would not signal failure, but regeneration, fresh starts and a successful decision to give myself and my children space to breathe and be free.

The next morning it hit me on another level. I had been living as an abused woman. I had to claim the victim title in order to fully accept the reality. For the same reason many people need to see the bodies of their deceased loved ones to truly believe they're dead, I needed to stand in the truth that I was a victim of domestic violence in order to move forward with confidence.

I took another seashell stroll. While my footprints faded into the softened salty sand, I contemplated the many descriptors I didn't want, but could throw in my profile: abuse victim, autistic mom, soon-to-be-divorcee, single mom, formerly eating disordered, rape victim. I walked with loved ones through substance abuse and mental health crises. I'd lived with anxiety and depression. I'd grieved the death of my dad at too young an age. I didn't know what any of those things were supposed to feel like, but I could claim all of those titles. Those experiences made me who I am. It was heavy. And oddly freeing. I'd faced so much. I could face developing a life on my own.

At that moment, I noticed a weird bump coming out of the sand just a few yards away. Expecting it to be a false alarm I went over and tried to pick it up. It was definitely a part of a shell, and it was definitely not budging. I dug around it and dug some more. Eventually I pulled out a conch shell that was not just three inches long, like the one I'd been so pleased to find the day before, but at least three to four inches in diameter and a good seven to eight inches long. Intact. Regeneration. Rebirth. Clearing negative, oppressive, evil energy away. I could do this. I could be free.

I returned from the trip ready to have the conversation. The conversation in which we would check in with each other and determine next steps. While I felt confident and secure and at peace, I also continued to experience the cognitive dissonance and confusion.

One moment we'd be laughing and joking together and I'd wonder if I misjudged him.

The next moment one of my children Face Timed me in a hushed voice saying they'd had a bad dream but were afraid to wake up their dad.

He'd follow through with something I'd asked him to do and I'd think he'd changed.

He'd be intolerant of my youngest's difficulty during the transitions.

My kids would share a fun story and ways they thought dad changed.

One kid would say they didn't know how to talk to their dad about wanting him to engage in play in a different way. The other kid would say, "There's no point, he doesn't listen anyway."

With every swing back and forth my own confusion would reignite. Not necessarily confusion over what I wanted my next step to be. I wanted a divorce and I knew that wasn't going to change, but confusion over what kind of a man he actually was.

We'd set a date in March to have the actual, big conversation. I'd said I didn't want to talk about it before then. He ignored that request and brought it up "just to get an idea of what I'm leaning toward." I told him I didn't want to talk about it until the time we'd scheduled. He started crying and telling me that he missed me and didn't want us to end. With all the grey stoning I could muster, I flatly told him that I just didn't know how I could trust him again.

The date in March came. Before I could utter a word, he spoke.

"I've been thinking about it. You said you can't trust me. So, the decision has been made, right? We can't have a marriage when you can't trust me."

I agreed and we decided we'd both reflect on how we wanted the divorce to proceed and figure out more permanent living arrangements.

He walked out and my friend walked in. She asked how it went.

"He basically made the decision without making the decision. It worked well for him. He didn't have to actually be the one who wanted to stay, but he also didn't have to be the one who decided to leave since he said it was because I couldn't trust him."

She asked how I felt.

"Relief and trepidation."

The decision had been voiced and he seemed agreeable, but for twenty years he also seemed supportive and like he cared. He used the circular wording to take responsibility without taking responsibility. I feared what it would look like when actual division of material things began. I feared what retribution he might enact. I was relieved it was beginning and I'd never have to live with him again.

"I'm gonna need to move into the basement."

"Excuse me?!" I think my jaw may have actually dropped.

Apparently the guy he had been living with planned to sell his house. Real estate moved fast and furious in those days and he expected the home to sell and close within a month.

"I won't have anywhere to go at the end of the month."

"I am not comfortable with you being in the basement and I think that'd be really confusing for the kids," I repeated the words I spoke two months earlier.

"I don't have any other options."

"I am not comfortable with you being in the basement and I think that'd be really confusing for the kids. Especially since we haven't lived together. They've known it was just a separation and if you move back in permanently it may give them false hope that we're getting back together."

"Since we're going to be separating finances, there's no way we can afford hotel rooms."

My insides churned and my brain argued with itself.

He's the father of my kids. He'd definitely make me the bad guy in their eyes if I refuse him a place to stay. He raped me. He doesn't have anyone else; he did leave his entire country and family for me. He is a narcissist that pushes boundaries; I cannot give into this or he'll only cross more boundaries. He'll just go and stay in a hotel and wrack up credit card debt that we will have to split during the divorce. I do not feel safe with him in the home. It already still feels heavy with his presence when I know he'd been sleeping in the same bed just the night before.

Despite all that messiness creating chaos throughout my insides, I embodied the grey stone.

"I am not comfortable with you being in the basement and I think it'd be really confusing for the kids."

Of course I knew the look, but it had never been quite as dark and threatening before. He closed the distance just a little, just enough that I felt less safe, but not enough that it was obvious. He always left room for plausible deniability. Had I mentioned it, he would have claimed he was only adjusting his body position. But, the look, the two steps forward. To the well-trained eye there was no mistaking what he was doing. The grey stoning was working. He wasn't getting his way. His narcissistic innards felt injured. He was at risk for losing control and therefore I felt at risk.

Through gritted teeth and a contemptuous sneer he growled something about not going to sleep in his car and that I was being ridiculous for expecting him to be homeless.

He turned and strutted out.

I'd forgotten that strut. When I first met him at camp, he'd strut every time he moved. So much so that I talked to him about how it made him look. He stopped strutting. Until he felt threatened. When he felt threatened or wanted others around him to know their place, the strut would return.

He strutted out and I went to my room, shut the door, and sat on the edge of the bed. Then I moved to the floor because the last place I wanted to be was sitting on the bed where I'd been repeatedly assaulted.

I breathed. I congratulated myself for grey stoning. I cried. I texted my friends. They encouraged me and reinforced the truth that it was not my responsibility to make sure he had someplace to stay. I'd been taking care of him for decades, I no longer needed to.

Those things helped. Of course they helped. Without skills to manage the anxiety, some medications to help with that, and my friends who would speak truth, my story would be so much different. Even with all those supports in place it was a daily struggle. Every time he pushed or crossed a boundary, I felt anxious and questioned if I was being fair. I'm sure he knew that. That's part of the narcissist's arsenal. I had to remind myself of that. Every exhausting day I needed to remind myself of the game.

It felt pretty scummy to play the game. It went against my nature. Being a perfect target for a narcissist—a person with the traits of compassion, empathy, generosity, intelligence, introspection, mercy and forgiveness—part of my nature was to assume the best of people. To believe in humankind's good will. To reframe poor behavior within the context of past trauma.

A psychic once told me that my energy center is Divine Truth. I'm not sure what I think about psychics, but this resonated with me to my core. I choose to seek truth, speak the truth and help others see the truth. I become infuriated when truth is disregarded. Truth guides the ways in which I interact with the world. I don't believe that human beings can fully understand all the universe's secrets, but I will forever seek truth.

I had to swallow my desire to be fully upfront with him. I knew it would be manipulated and used against me as we negotiated the terms of the divorce. I had to resist the urge to shout out to everyone that he's a narcissist and not someone to be trusted. I would only appear to be the crazy, embittered one. I had to endure his subtle, but active, smear campaign and trust that the people who knew me would see the truth. I had to accept that people who walked away from me weren't people I wanted around anyway.

My friends shared things he told them as he tried to sway them into seeing his perspective and regard me as a bad person. He told my friends that it was my fault we were splitting up and that I wouldn't even give us another chance. He said he wanted to go to counseling and I refused. He said he was making efforts and I just wouldn't give him any credit or any opportunities to repair the relationship. He told my friends that I unreasonably forced him out of the home and that he would be homeless. He anti-laughed and said "She actually thinks I'm a narcissist. I was worried about it, so I asked all of my coworkers. They all laughed and said there's no way I could be a narcissist."

These were the things he was saying to people we were both close to, so I knew the things he said to others had to have been worse.

I know that he played victim with my children and gave the appearance of remorse. Part of me still hopes he was actually remorseful and changed his parenting ways. And whether that's continued cognitive dissonance or not, I have to believe it for the sake of my kids and to be able to say goodbye to them every weekend, leaving them in the care of their father. During the separation, though, I could feel at least two of my children being pulled into the caregiving role. I could hear them protecting his emotions and providing reassurance. Things that a child should not be doing for a parent.

I'm assuming he'd phrased things in ways that intimated I was leaving him. My kids are smart, so I don't think he would have straight out said it was my fault, but I know my youngest two approached me and asked, through tears, why I was divorcing daddy. They reassured me he'd changed. My youngest even called him bad dad and new dad. I wanted to shout the truth to them, make them see all that I could see, but their relationship with their dad is their relationship with their dad and they love him. I told them that I really hoped he had changed, that I hoped he could be the kind of dad they need him to be. I told them that there were a lot of years and hurts and times when he said he was going to change in our marriage and he didn't. I told them neither of us could be happy together anymore. I reinforced that if divorcing was going to be the thing that actually changed him to be a better dad, then it was worth it.

They could have arrived to those conclusions on their own, but having overheard some of the not-joking jokes he'd made in my presence, I also know he had an influence. "Mommy's just glad to be rid of me. No, no . . . I'm joking!" "Oh sorry! I know it's your time with the kids and you want me out of the house, I'm almost ready." "Here's the debit card. I figured you'd enjoy cutting mine up."

I trusted in my relationship with my kids. They know I deeply love them and will do anything for them. I know they feel safe with me and can be their full selves with me. We all felt moments of lightness and fun in the midst of all the struggle. I noticed the difference and the lightness when it was just the four of us and I'm certain they could feel it, too.

They saw me dancing in the kitchen and heard me singing. Their mom slowly gained a little more energy. I laughed and joked and threw cheese at my daughter to see if it'd stick (it was a TikTok trend at the time). I'm not sure that any of them had any recollection of this version of me. Of the real me. The me that had my soul intact and felt lighthearted and joyful.

There was a time in mid spring when the four of us went out for a hike. I hadn't appropriately calculated for the shade of the evergreens surrounding the trail, and so while most of the snow had melted, the trail continued to be icy. We looked at the little hill in front of us, looked at each other, agreed we'd be skating instead of hiking and took off anyway. We slid and fell and lost our balance. We made weird noises and laughed and made jokes about not being able to get back up the hill and being stuck in the woods until a thaw came. I nearly cried. It was the first time in a LONG time that something went off plan and we laughed about it and enjoyed it together. No oppositional, pissed off energy or negative comments the whole time. No adult saying it wasn't a good idea, but refusing to make a decision about whether to proceed or not. We simply enjoyed the moment.

It was those moments that gave me hope and kept me going. Those moments kept my head in the game so my children and I could have that sense of light, love and freedom. I knew we had a long way to go before it became the norm, and I knew many moments of anger, sadness and terror stood between us and that daily light. But I could see it and feel it coming.

I knew it was coming and I trusted that my kids could feel me loving them well. Still, his manipulations, smearing and attempts to alienate me terrified me.

They terrified me so much I felt nervous going to my van in the darkened parking lot at night. I felt anxious filling up with gas when others weren't around. I worried I was being followed or recorded or spied on. I didn't know how far he could take it and I didn't want to take chances.

I'm pretty sure I had nothing to worry about. His desperation to keep the public appearances positive prevented him from doing anything too drastic. He wasn't a physically violent person. I've also heard so many stories in which coercive controllers become physically violent for the first time when their victim is leaving.

It certainly didn't help that he made a few thinly veiled threats.

"You changed the locks? What? Afraid I'm gonna come in and just assault you sometime?"

The most chilling occurred shortly after the COVID-19 pandemic started. He coughed, and from a nearby room my daughter shouted out, "Covid!"

He turned to me and with his not-joking, joking smile he said, "I bet you kinda wish it was. I get Covid and die, insurance money for you!"

I rolled my eyes and said, "Oh, c'mon," to indicate that no, I did not wish him dead.

He looked incredulous and said, "What? Like it hasn't crossed your mind."

And then he paused, looked me straight in the eyes and said, "I know I've thought about it." He turned his head and body and called out for our daughter with a smile on his face.

Whether the physical threat of harm was real, psychological, or even just imagined, it didn't really matter. I felt unsafe. Our brains are pretty amazing, but they don't understand the difference between psychological threat and physical threat. My day job is filled with advocacy and justification that our psychological selves cannot be minimized in favor of our physical selves. We have somehow determined to treat them separately, though they are intertwined in ways it's impossible to put into words. Our brains, bodies and whole selves understand that psychological danger is just as real as physical danger. Our brains understand all stress to be life-threatening. I'd been through enough psychological torment to be living in a constant state of high alert. The degree of physical threat didn't matter. My brain, body, emotions and soul were all living in a life-threatening situation.

Sometimes I gaslit myself by telling myself I was overreacting, too sensitive and being ridiculous. Sometimes my brain carried me down an anxious path filled with all the worst-case scenarios and made me believe them. I was exhausted from being on high alert, from the adrenaline coursing through my body, from the ever-present internal dialogue in which I tried to work out what was real and what wasn't. I felt exhausted, but my soul wasn't weary. I wanted to sleep for five hundred and two days, but I didn't want to melt into the floor and sink into oblivion. This was an exhaustion for which there was healing, rest and recovery. This was an exhaustion accompanied by hope.

I'd read somewhere on a social media platform that we shouldn't confuse manipulation and emotional abuse with an anger management problem. The article pointed out that if this person can hold their temper out in public and only loses control at home, they can manage their anger just fine. And it's true. Unleashing of rage and intimidation only at home is an intentional attempt to establish coercive control.

An incident with our friend drove this home to me. We we were all sitting together. This was sometime before his official non-decision decision to divorce, but after we had separated. He had to print something. He grabbed the document from the printer and lost his shit. It had printed crookedly. To be fair, he lost his shit only in terms of ranting and raving, but this was by no means the most intense I'd seen him. My friend and I sat quietly and just looked at him. He cleared his throat, stood up and walked out of the room.

My friend turned to me and it was then that I noticed the shock on her face. Her eyes were wide and she swallowed hard. She said, "Wow. That was intense. I've never seen him like that."

It was my turn to look shocked.

"Really?"

"Seriously, Heather. I've never seen him so angry or flip out like that about anything. What *was* that?!"

"My daily life," I said.

He came back quietly and apologized. He said he was not sure why he overreacted like that. We moved on.

Internally, however, I continued to sit in shock. I couldn't think of a single time when he apologized for a similar mini-rage, or even for a big rage. There were times he'd fauxpologize to one of the kids, especially when he lost it with my daughter. But a true taking of accountability? I couldn't remember a single time.

My mind continued to digest the revelation that our friend had never seen this side of him before. They'd spent a lot of time together. He considered her his friend first and even accused me of stealing her from him. She'd never seen a mini tantrum of his? It was such a part of my normal world that I just assumed everyone saw glimpses of it. The realization that he reserved his darker side only for the kids and me reinforced the intentionality. All of the excuses I'd made for him were completely unfounded.

No incident solidified my understanding better than what happened the day we made decisions about all the stuff and things that accumulated over the course of a couple of decades.

I remember it distinctly. I stood in my bedroom; he stood in the doorway to the master bath. He'd decided that I should keep the house and he'd find a different place to live. He told me I could keep the bed. I told him he might as well take it because I wasn't going to be using it. No way in hell would I begin my freedom by sleeping in the bed in which I'd been raped. I also told him I'd buy our oldest a new bed and he could take that one.

"How are you affording all this?" he accused.

I shrugged my shoulders and said I was fine.

"Your mom or aunt must have given you money?" he asked.

I flatly said, "Nope."

I could feel the narcissistic injury increasing and his tone became just a hint wilder. "That doesn't make sense? How are you planning to buy all this new furniture while I barely have enough to pay my portion of the bills?"

I flatly said, "I don't know." To myself I said, "Because I don't have a parasite leaching off my hard work anymore."

"You must have been squirreling money away this whole time. Seriously, have you been stealing money?"

This is called projecting. It's a favorite of narcissists world-wide. They take their own traits and label you with them. If a narc accuses you of something, consider it a confession of their own behavior. Early in the marriage he'd repeatedly accuse me of being selfish. At one point in the separation he accused me of being the narcissist. And at this point in time he accused me of stealing his money.

My grey stoned self just said, "Nope."

He walked into the bathroom with disgust, then quickly turned back around. The anger and accusatory face had faded. He closed the gap and softly said, "I'm sorry. Of course you aren't. That's not who you are. I'm just so stressed out by all of this and I'm worried about the money and . . . "

He faded off and started to sob.

I stood there grey stoned.

"This isn't what I want," he cried.

"Okay," I grey stoned.

He sobbed.

I stood there.

In an instant he stopped crying and started threatening. When I say stopped crying, I mean his face was dry. There was a sob sound one second and then The Look the next.

There was no transition. He shifted tactics. He began to yell, to rant.

I can't remember what he was saying. I was blocking out his words so that I didn't react. It must have worked, because he pretty quickly left the room and the conversation.

I stood stunned. This grey stoning shit really worked. And, his whirling hurricane of approaches were all textbook and so clear to me. He started with accusations and projection. When that didn't work, he shifted into playing victim and trying to appeal to my empathetic side. When that didn't work, he resorted to rage and fear. When that didn't work, he left.

I think of those ten or fifteen minutes regularly. Any time I wonder if I've read him wrong, I remember those few minutes. Those few minutes, and the times he continued to touch my body in my sleep despite being asked not to on numerous occasions.

As suddenly as he'd told me he needed to move back into the basement, he stopped talking about it. Fearful that I would find him squatting down there one night, I asked about it. He would give ambiguous responses, like, "He may not be selling it now" or "I think I've figured something out." Another favorite of narcissists, is to give non-answer answers.

Since my kids wouldn't be going there and it appeared he wasn't going to be in my basement, I didn't push it and didn't really care what he figured out.

Figuring out the more permanent living situation became the next focus after we'd decided to divorce. He said I could have the house. I wasn't sure if I wanted the house or not, but I did the math and could afford it, so fine. Then the kids could have some consistency and I didn't have to move.

We'd decided he'd move out in the beginning of May.

May approached and I asked a few times what he'd found. I knew he was going to drag this out. That was one of the downsides of me staying in the house. it meant the actual separation was on his terms and timeline.

Eventually, at the last minute, he'd told me that he found a great fit. He'd talked to the kids and they were excited about it.

He planned to rent the upstairs, two-bedroom unit of a duplex. His friend rented the downstairs two-bedroom unit. The friend also nested while divorcing her husband and their schedules would work well together. During the week, he would stay in his upstairs unit and when he had the kids, he'd have access to both units. He planned on having our barely fifteen-year-old son and our twelve-year-old autistic daughter upstairs. The seven-year-old would be in the extra bedroom downstairs and he'd sleep in his friend's bed downstairs.

"But, they're separate units, right?" I asked, confused.

"Well, yeah, but they share the main entrance, so we'll leave the interior unit doors unlocked and just lock the exterior door. It'll be like one big house."

"But what if our daughter has a meltdown?"

"Her brother will be there."

"That's a lot to put on a fifteen-year-old who is also having to adjust to his parents' divorcing."

"It'll be fine. I'd be right downstairs, and mostly we'll be upstairs anyway, we'll just be downstairs to sleep."

"But they each have their own kitchens? Basically our teen and autistic pre-teen will be living in their own apartment."

He continued to try to convince me. I continued to be skeptical at best. It also seemed really weird to me that his female friend felt comfortable with him sleeping in her bed every weekend.

That piece of the puzzle fell into place fairly quickly. For legit reasons that I cannot legally discuss, I needed to look through our call logs. Predictably, a number kept popping up on his call log at very odd times and with very long call durations. Hours of phone calls. Every day he had the kids. Maybe a sporadic call to that number on the days he didn't have the kids, but they were very few and far between. Calls at four in the morning. Calls at midnight. Calls when he was supposed to be putting the kids to bed.

They'd started sometime in February. They accelerated in frequency and duration pretty quickly in March. I noticed that, in March, the calls took place across all days of the week, then they shifted to only the days he had the kids.

Naturally I googled the number, knowing it'd be a female. And, sure enough, she had the same name as his friend with the downstairs duplex unit.

PART THREE: FREEDOM

I felt so many things all at once. My gut lurched with the familiar pang of betrayal. My compassion soared for this unsuspecting woman who was his backup supply. Narcissists frequently have another target in the wings, just in case their primary supply dries up. I felt weary over another "thing" to process. The anger of a proactive mama bear coursed through my veins as I considered he wanted to involve our children in her life. Satisfaction puffed my chest as I realized he'd most likely been living with her since March. I knew I'd detected something strange about his story. Gratitude brought peace to my soul as I knew he'd have less reason to make the divorce difficult or antagonize me now that he had his new supply.

Around this same time my oldest started talking to a female friend nightly and for hours. When asked, he would insist that they were "just friends." During one of the transitions, his dad mentioned it to me with a sly grin that our oldest would most likely have a girlfriend soon.

I said, "Yeah, a dude doesn't talk to a girl on the phone every day for hours at a time unless he's into her and they're going to be hooking up."

He laughed and adamantly agreed. I thought of the call log and grinned that, unbeknownst to him, I'd caught him in his own trap.

I'd later learned that a few of my friends knew this woman. My friends reported that she has a beautiful, empathic, compassionate soul, with all the traits a narc targets.

While trying to convince me of the awesome duplex arrangement, he assured me that this woman was just a friend going through something similar. We'd had a discussion about bringing new people into our children's lives. He advocated for dating someone for six months before introducing them to our kids. I'd later learned that she helped him move out. The first weekend my kids spent with their father at his new place, she spent the day with them. Their friendship miraculously grew closer a few weeks after our divorce finalized and they began dating. He moved in with her three months later.

I'd be lying if I said none of it bothered me as a woman who had been so recently married to him. But I had no interest in resuming our relationship, so I healed from that aspect fairly quickly. His involving her with our kids so quickly and being so devious about it enraged me. What a fine example for our children. You start dating someone and then move in with them three months later.

Another difficult aspect of this relationship was the relationship my daughter developed with her. I became grateful for this woman's presence. I know that their dad had to keep up a good show for her. I was glad they had a mothering figure in their lives when I couldn't be there. She, of course, wasn't their mom and so their comfort level wasn't secure with her. My daughter would talk about doing nails and hair, and all the mother-daughter girl things. I felt envy and anger. I wanted to have those things with my daughter, but instead I was making her do therapy exercises, bringing her to doctor appointments and holding space for her while she was melting down. She and her younger brother were melting down every Sunday night when I got them back. They'd be fine as they said goodbye to their father, and then the huge emotions began. I gladly took it and walked with them through it, often with my own tears flowing and feeling helpless and tired. This other woman got the sunny side of mothering while I was too busy cleaning up the emotional refuse of my children.

I have spoken with my daughter about this, and she understands in her own way. I truly want her to have a positive relationship with her stepmom. And I want to have the challenges and the joys of positive relationships with my children. As healing has progressed, we definitely experience more laughs and joy than sadness and emotional spewing.

Back in May of 2020, however, their dad wanted this odd living situation in the duplex. I'd run it past my therapist, my son's therapist, my friends and family, and not a single person thought it was a good idea. Knowing I could be biased, I needed that confirmation.

May approached and he began spinning his stories. They thought it'd be ready for May 1st, but they needed to do some work on it, so it'll be May 15th. Fine, I said. Out by May 15th, whether this particular situation is ready or not.

For some reason my child, his dad and I were all in his room at the same time and the topic of the duplex came up. I told him I was really uncomfortable with the arrangement, and wanted to physically walk through the place before I agreed it would be safe for our children.

I remember feeling very hesitant to talk about it in front of my son, and I wish I could remember how I got drawn into it, but it was a time when I wasn't able to grey stone.

He was standing in the doorway; I couldn't get out and the conversation continued in front of my son.

"Why are you so against this place?! They think it's cool!"

"Let's all look at it and figure it out. I can't stop you from making the decision to move there, but I don't think it's unreasonable for me to look at it. You're talking about putting two of our kids, one with autism, in a separate unit than you. I want to make sure it's safe."

"It's a four bedroom for the price of two. A whole house. I wouldn't be able to afford this otherwise."

"Like I said, I just want to make sure it's safe."

He turned The Look on me and said, "Do you really think I'd take my kids to live someplace that's unsafe?!"

Yes. I did. His motivation to save money and be closer to his new supply seemed clear to me. I couldn't say that in front of my child.

"I'm simply asking to see it first."

This was a phrase he used a lot. "I'm simply asking." Or, "I simply want." It's a form of gaslighting and manipulating. It communicates that you think the other person is making a big deal out of a small request. I intentionally used that phrase, and I'm pretty sure he knew it.

I don't know how it ended. But, obviously, we left my son's room. I later went and checked in with him and apologized. I said that conversation never should have happened in front of him. Like the oldest, overly responsible, hold it all in young man he is, he said it was fine.

I never saw the duplex. I continued to voice my concerns.

He continued to tell me that we couldn't get in to look at it because of the construction. May 15th moved to June 1st. I reflected that he kept pushing the boundaries, which has been a recurring problem. He yelled, "What do you want me to do about it? It's construction!" I wasn't sure if the construction was actually happening or not.

June first approached. "I'm going to need more time," he said. "I just realized the unit won't have air conditioning. Our daughter can't live in a place without air conditioning."

If it wasn't so predictable and there wasn't an excuse for everything, it'd be more believable. But, he lies, and therefore I have no reason to believe this wasn't a whole pack of lies, too.

"June 15th. That's it. If you don't have a place in which the kids can live with you, not a problem. They can stay with me until you do. But you need to be out by June 15th."

"How am I supposed to find a place in two weeks?"

"That is not my responsibility. Had you looked for a regular place from the beginning, you'd have been living there for a month by now. The kids will be taken care of. June 15th."

Needless to say, he wasn't a fan.

He threatened to just move back in, declaring that there wasn't anything I could do about it because it was his house too.

He told me I was being unreasonable.

He played victim.

He tried being nice to me and talking about how much he missed me.

He cried about being a bad dad.

I grey stoned through it all.

And then the date kept creeping closer and I needed a new tactic. I couldn't legally kick him out because he did own the house as much as I did. Instead, I jumped into the game. If I could make him feel like he's winning, maybe he'd finally leave.

I told him that it was really rough living at my mom's and going back and forth every weekend. I told him that I really needed the space to myself so we can begin moving forward and the kids don't have to be in limbo anymore.

It worked.

He got to be the hero, put on his fake empathy and say, "I didn't realize it was so difficult with your mom. I'll find something as soon as I can."

He got to win. He was staying with his new girlfriend and I was miserable at my mom's.

He got to save the day and be nice in an attempt to keep up the good appearance to me and the kids.

He got to be the good dad who rescued his children from unending ambiguity.

He also got to have about three weeks without the children. While he puts on the face that he's an involved dad, he has on only one occasion asked for extra time with them. Their stepmom has asked for extra time with them more than he has. In the three years since the decree was finalized, he hasn't taken his annual week for a vacation or staycation with them. Moving and not being able to get into the place right away gave him the perfect opportunity to be child-free without looking like he wanted to be.

As he prepared to move, we did the final walkthrough of all the possessions we'd accumulated through the years. It was gross. I had a notebook in hand. We went room by room. As though he were an entitled millionaire redecorating his second home, he pointed at things and said, "I'll take that and that. I don't want that; you can have it." I don't know what I'd expected, but the lack of consideration for my thoughts, his inability to actually talk through this division, the oozing entitlement and arrogance left me with the need to shower.

He moved out June 15th. I felt victorious. I felt free. I felt like I could stop just healing and start moving forward.

The kids moved in and began alternating homes the second weekend in July.

That same weekend, I painted my bedroom. I assembled my new bed, complete with headboard, footboard and frame. I'd wanted a designed and coordinated bedroom throughout our entire marriage. He never agreed to spend the money on it. At one point I took out $500 and bought second hand furniture, some paint and some lumber. While he was at work, I redecorated our bedroom in a style he would like and made a faux headboard against the wall. He had no idea. He expressed suitable surprise and gratitude. On the second night he pointed out things he didn't like about it, but I didn't really like those things either, so I took no offense.

But this second weekend of July 2020, I had only myself to please. I chose the linens I liked and designed around that. I created a cozy sanctuary that felt like Heather. I saged the room. I cleaned from floor to ceiling. I put the bed on a different wall. I danced and laughed and worked and cried and, in the end, I felt home, safe and secure in my own room for the first time.

During our marriage, I had created all of the home decorating and design projects with my own blood, sweat and tears. He'd help when I told him what to do, but for the most part, he'd read, sleep, game, feed the children and keep the children away from the room I was working on. I did everything else, and I enjoyed it. As a therapist I don't often get to see a concrete beginning, middle and end in my work. The occasional home project satisfies that need.

Working on my room felt different, though. It gave me confidence and a fresh start. It reminded me who I am and that I'm going to be ok. As I reflect on it now, it was also the first home project that was one hundred percent entirely about me. I was giving myself a feeling of luxury and safety. And though the work was hard, the reward was worth it. There's a line from a Kelly Clarkson song that goes, "I know I've got this cause I've had it all along." Hell, yeah!

The eight months from when he moved out until the divorce finalized were not what I'd expected. I hated leaving my children with him, getting their hushed calls in the middle of the nights, knowing I couldn't stand as barrier between them and The Look. I intended to use that time to get my work done.

After about three months I wondered when I'd actually be productive on Saturdays. I couldn't get myself out of bed. I slept and glazed over and watched tv and slept. My friend encouraged compassion and gentleness. I'd been living in trauma for twenty years; it was going to take more than a couple months for it to clear my system. I hadn't been able to sleep soundly and safely for years. My body was catching up.

I managed to do just enough to keep life and work afloat. I got some things done on Sundays and greeted my children with love, open arms and emotional safety every Sunday night. We'd make our way through the meltdowns and begin Mondays fresh. We'd play games and laugh and learn to enjoy life as a foursome. Then Fridays would come. I'd work, they'd go to their dad's and Saturdays I'd collapse and rest.

I don't know how long it took, but eventually my energy returned. I needed less rest and more activity. I could be productive again and even grew excited about creative endeavors and projects. Just as my soul deteriorated one paper cut at a time over years, it also rejuvenated one breath, one laugh, one moment of joy at a time.

His shenanigans, and attempts to control me and my life continued. I had to take the lead on filing for divorce. I filed in September. Instead of paying for someone to serve him, my attorney mailed them. He didn't receive them the first time because he gave me the wrong unit number. He didn't receive them the second time because mail in his complex often went missing and someone must have stolen them. The third set I served to him directly when he dropped off the kids. Miraculously the paperwork showed up in his mailbox the following week.

That same month I booked a cabin at the camp my family regularly attends. The same camp where I led the autism camp. The same camp where my trip toward freedom began. The kids and I trekked the three hours there, service dog in tow. We talked about how we'd let the weekend be what it needed to be. And it certainly was. Camp created a space for all of us to sit with our emotions and release them. We yelled, we cried, we gave to each other, we sang and we healed. It wasn't the last time we'd do any of these things, but it seemed to mark a turning point. We cared for each other in ways we hadn't before. We celebrated when I cooked burgers on a grill for the first time ever and they were edible. We allowed each person to fully feel and be who they needed to be. No chastising, no forcing, no intolerance. My daughter put aside her own wants and insisted we continue hiking because it was the one thing I wanted to do. That was a first. It was hard and it was beautiful.

It also seemed fitting. I began my family at a little camp in Maine, when a narcissist played Prince Charming and swept me off my feet. Decades later, war-torn and battle bruised, I showed back up to a camp and began recognizing that my fairy tale had been anything but happily ever after. And now, with my beautiful children, I listened to the crickets, looked at the millions of stars twinkling overhead, and knew we were writing a new and glorious story.

The story continues. It is not and never will be a fairytale, but it *is* a magnificent mess. I once heard that coparenting with a narcissist is much more difficult than single parenting: it's single parenting with an elephant sitting on your chest. I couldn't agree more. But, I'm stronger, wiser and living in an environment of light. I'd much rather coparent with the elephant on my chest than in my home.

It took some navigating to come to an agreement on the terms of the divorce, but we did, and thankfully, without too much expense or time lost. On February 10, 2021 the court granted the divorce.

I don't entirely know what my future holds, but I do know I will be free.

Acknowledgments

This was a story decades in the making and years in the writing. I could not have had the courage, time, and wherewithal to complete the project without the support of so many.

First, my three biological children. I am regularly impressed with their maturity, wisdom, and love. Without their ability to understand that my relationship with their father is separate from theirs, this book would never have existed. They understand and support the need for me to speak the truth of my experiences and trusted me to do so in a way that respected their own voices and stories. I am so honored to be their mom.

My safe, loving, and encouraging husband. His dedication to this book rivaled my own. He retreated with me while I wrote the most difficult parts, tolerating my pain so that it could be raw and shared on the page and then immediately held me in his arms when the writing was done but the emotions were not. His mantra "the world needs your words" gave me strength, eased my anxieties, and kept me focused on my purpose.

My best friend, Rachel, witnessed this story first hand through the decades and was the first person I trusted to read the manuscript. Without her thirty-four years of unwavering support this story would have been so very different.

I never doubt that my mom will be my safety net and provide me the unconditional love that all people should get from their mothers. Again, without her, this story would have been so very different.

Maryann and the team at Armin Lear took my story and made it a beautiful book, and in the process made me a better writer. Thank you.

We have never met, but the words, wisdom, and experiences of so many thought leaders truly changed my life. Through their work I learned the narcissist's playbook and not only saw my own life more clearly, but have been able to help countless others understand their experiences. Thank you to Debbie Mirza, Helena Knowlton, George Simon, the Real Crime Profile podcast hosts (Jim Clemente, Laura Richards, & Lisa Zambetti), Rebecca Zung, and Dr. Ramani Durvasula.

And finally, I would be remiss if I didn't acknowledge the millions of women and men who are being targeted by their own narcissists. You are not alone. You are not crazy. You are stronger than you think and everyday I pray you find your way out.

About the Author

Heather Boorman-Morris, MSW, LCSW has dedicated her life to ease suffering and nurture healing through sharing her personal stories and professional wisdom as an author, speaker, teacher, and therapist. Her writings include articles and book contributions on neurodiversity, mental health, and trauma recovery, as well as her first book The Gifted Kids Workbook. Heather teaches as an adjunct professor at the University of St Thomas and has provided therapy through her private practice for over fourteen years. Her favorite times are sitting around a table with the true love of her life and their four children, the food growing cold as laughter and light-hearted joy eclipse the task at hand.

www.ingramcontent.com/pod-product-compliance
Lightning Source LLC
Chambersburg PA
CBHW020330170426
43200CB00006B/329